TABLE OF CONTENTS

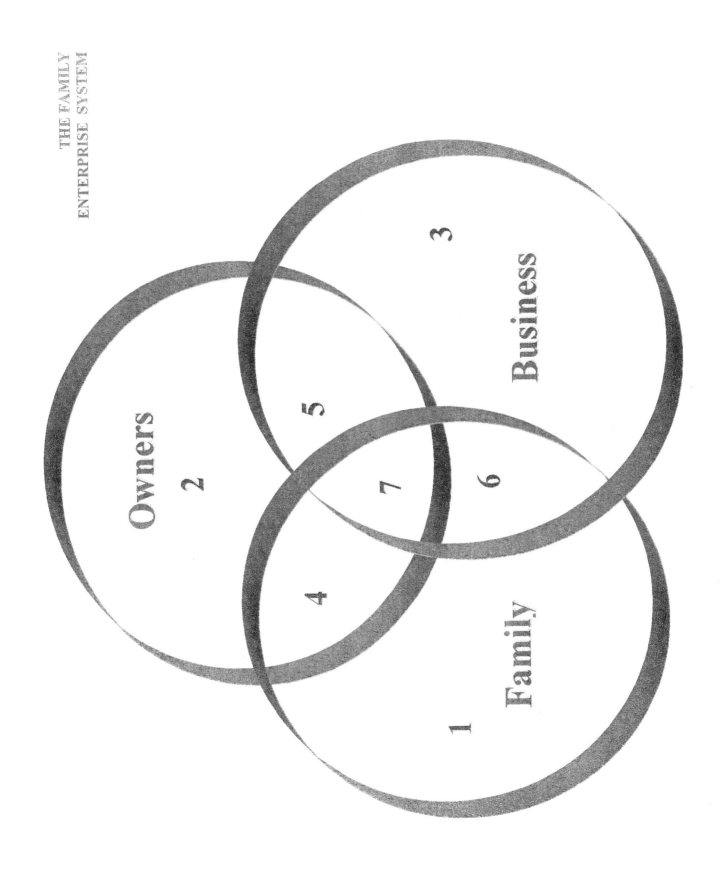

The Family Enterprise Systems

❖ 1. Family member not in the business, not an owner

❖ 2. Owner, not a family member nor working in the business

❖ 3. Working in the business, not a family member, not an owner

❖ 4. Family member who is an owner but not working in the business

❖ 5. Owner working in the business but not a family member

❖ 6. Family member working in the business

❖ 7. Family member working in the business who is also an owner

Family Business Systems: Glossary of Terms

Differentiation: The ability of an individual to distinguish between emotional and intellectual functioning. In relationships, the ability to maintain a solid, non-negotiable self and to take comfortable "I" positions. A primary yardstick of psychological health, according to Bowen's family systems theory. The differentiated person can risk genuine emotional closeness without undue anxiety.

Fusion: The quality of blending emotions and intellect so that one is unable to distinguish between the two. The degree to which mutually interconnected relationships are "stuck together." In fused relationships, none of the individuals can move independently of the others or the whole.

Enmeshment: An intense level of emotional closeness in families. The quality of being so interdependent emotionally that an individual's boundaries crumble and personal privacy is nonexistent.

Disengagement: A low level of emotional closeness in families. The quality of being so independent emotionally that individuals avoid supporting each other or sharing in each other's thoughts, decisions or actions.

Triangling: The process of bringing a third person into a two-person relationship in order to defuse the tension within the original dyad. Prevents direct resolution of conflict by the twosome.

Birth order: The tendency of one's position in the sequence of a family's childbirths to affect the roles and perceptions that the person carries through life. Other things being equal, persons who occupy the same relative position among their family's children will share common characteristics.

Sibling rivalry: A conflictual tendency that begins when children compete at a young age for their parents' love and attention, and can continue through the children's adult lives in the family business. While a certain amount of sibling rivalry can foster creativity and growth, it has a damaging impact if taken to extremes.

Emotional cutoff: Isolating oneself, withdrawing or running away from one's unresolved emotional attachments to parents in an effort to restart life in a new generation. While the cutoff process may feel like a declaration of independence, it in fact merely submerges unresolved emotional attachment to the parental family and leaves the individual as emotionally dependent as the one who never leaves home.

Source: Dr. Murray Bowen, Ph.D.

THE SON YOU WISH YOU HAD

Dynamic, young CPA, with over 14 years experience in aggressive management, marketing, tax and financial planning, seeks opportunity to learn & acquire an on-going small to medium sized business. If you own a company and wish to retire or reduce your workload, but have no heirs or replacements available, I may be your answer! I am honest, hard working and enjoy an excellent professional reputation. All terms and conditions will be REASONABLY NEGOTIATED. Please write in TOTAL CONFIDENCE to P.O. Box 670852, Marietta, GA 30066

"Then bit by bit, the kid took over."

BLOODIEST TAKOVER STRUGGLE I EVER WITNESSED

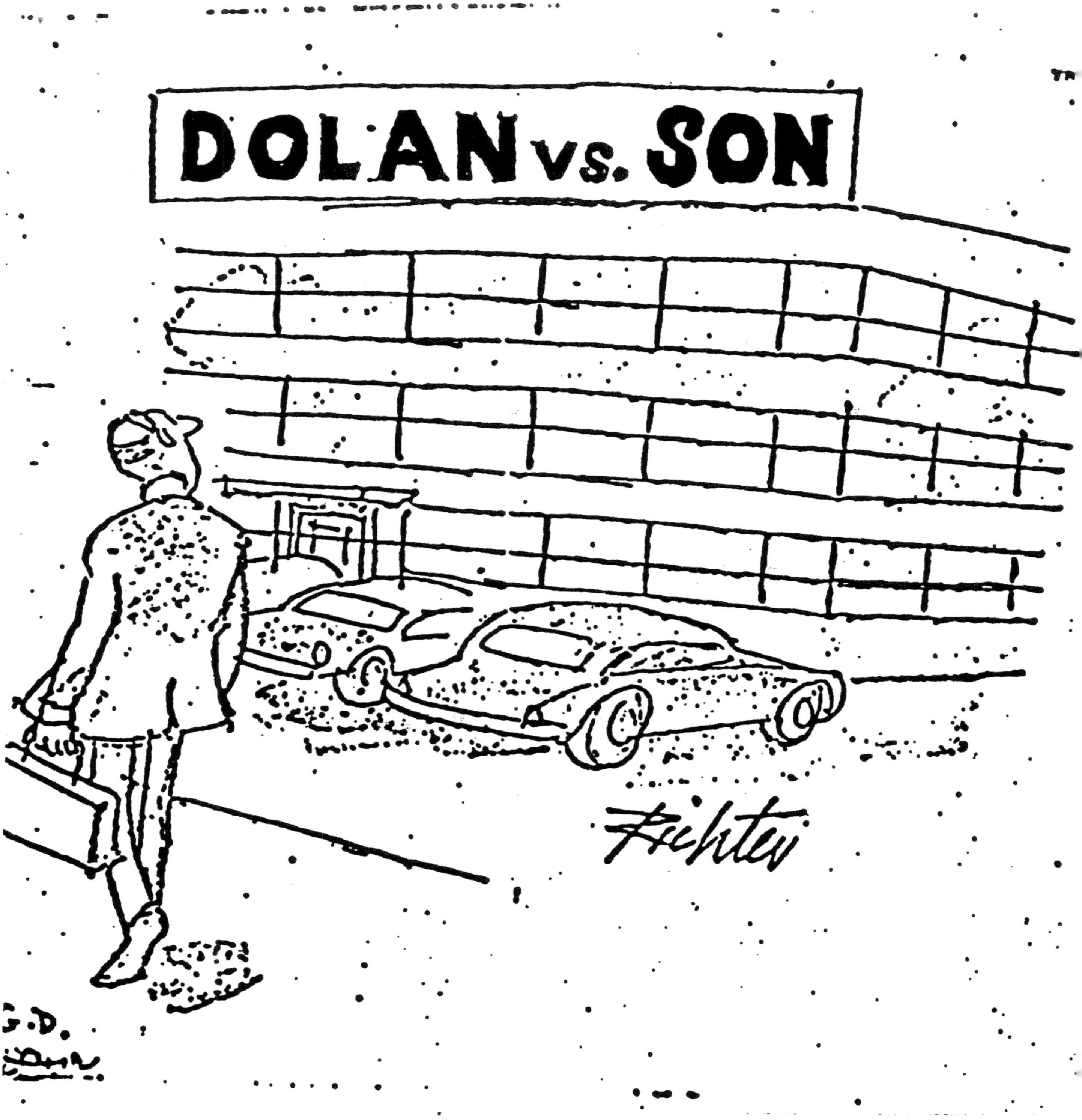
DOLAN vs. SON
Richter

What do you see?

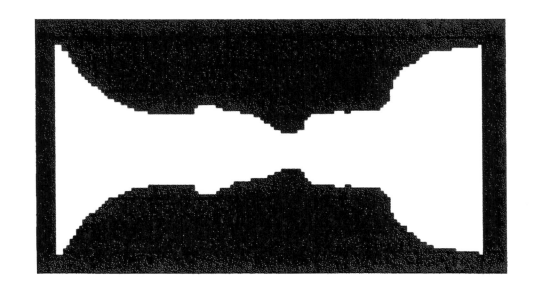

What do you see?

8

What do you see?

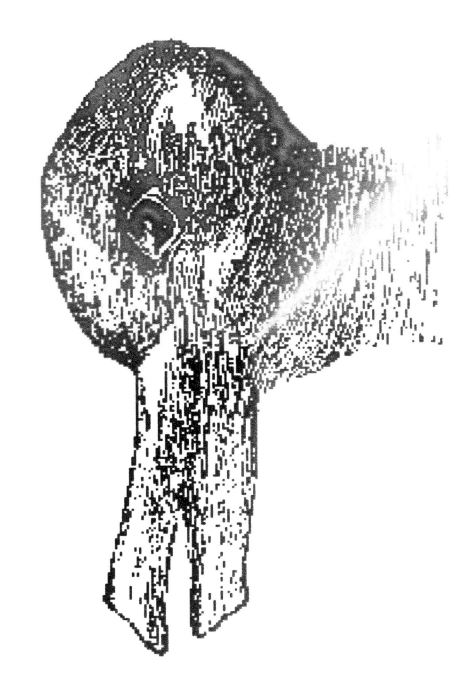

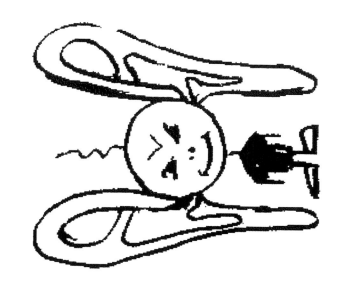

3 Levels of Listening

- ## Level I – Internal listening
  – focus on self

- ## Level II – Focused listening
  – focus on other

- ## Level III – Global listening
  – Focus on all senses

11

Improving Listening Skills

- Recognize everyone is having a different experience
- Create a climate where people are willing to express their own truth and learn from it
- Ask people to tell the truth about their experience – truly inquire
- Seek first to understand rather than to be understood
- Be present and engaged

12

FAMILY BUSINESS MANAGEMENT

The Confrontation Model

This model allows us to confront tough issues with courage, compassion, and skill. Learning is provoked and relationships are enriched.

Opening Statement:
Write your opening statement. Then answer all the questions and if possible actually have a conversation with the person you are having the issue with. Please no more than 2 pages if possible. Double spaced w/ cover sheet.

Your Opening Statement should:

1. Name the issue

2. Select a specific example that illustrates the behavior or situation you want to change.

3. Describe your emotions about this issue

4. Clarify what is at stake

5. Identify your contribution to the problem

6. Indicate your wish to resolve the issue

7. Invite your partner to respond

Interaction

8. Inquire into your partners views. Use paraphrasing and a perception check. Dig for full understanding; don't be satisfied with the surface. Make sure your partner knows that you fully understand and acknowledge his or her position and interests.

Resolution

9. What have we learned? Where are we now? Has anything been left unsaid that needs saying? What is needed for resolution? How can we move forward from here, given our new understanding?

10. Make a new agreement and determine how you will hold each other responsible for keeping it.

3

Getting Things Straight: Clear Communication and Conflict Resolution

"Some relationships work better than others. We all know people with whom we feel comfortable, secure, able to talk through a problem, and confident. With others we feel uncomfortable, frustrated, and mistrustful. We rarely understand why some relationships work well and others don't. We tend to accept the quality of a relationship as inevitable: 'That's the way it is. We just don't get along.' We blame problems on the other person and assume that there is little we can do to improve the way we interact.

"Although it takes two to have a relationship, it takes only one to change its quality. Just as we react to others, they react to us. By changing our behavior, we will change the way they react."

-Roger Fisher and Scott Brown, Getting Together

23

One of the most public family feuds in recent years was played out by the Bingham family of Louisville. The patriarch, Barry Sr., tried to resolve a feud between his son Barry Jr., manager of the family's newspaper and media business, and daughter Sallie, an owner who had been forced off the board of directors. Their conflict stemmed from old family feelings and went on for several years, ultimately forcing the sale of the business. The struggle has inspired several books, including one written by Sallie herself, and many of the intra-family messages in the feud were sent via letters to the editor in the family newspaper. The consensus of observers is that there were several ways that the feud could have been resolved short of a sale.

Barry Bingham Sr. was the third-generation heir who built the family newspaper holdings into a lucrative and well-respected empire. He, his wife Mary, and their three sons and two daughters led a storybook life of privilege. But their children's lives were marked by tragedy. The eldest son, Worth, talented, gregarious, and aggressive like his father, was expected to be the successor. His younger brother, Barry Jr., was devoted to him. But Worth's life was cut short by an accident in 1966, just two years after another accident killed his younger brother, Jonathan. In 1971, Barry Jr. was asked by his father to take over the family newspapers. That same year he contracted cancer, which was treated and went into remission.

Barry Jr. presided over a difficult era of declining profits in the newspaper business. While he was shyer than Worth and less prepared to be a business leader, Barry did a creditable job, although he was seen by many as aloof and demanding. In 1977 his sisters, Sallie and Eleanor, moved back to Louisville, and conflict began to erupt. Sallie felt like an outsider. Although close to her father, she had felt excluded from the strong bond between Barry Jr. and Worth when she was growing up. Barry Jr. and Sallie had not had much contact in many years, and were never close. She had been successful as a writer, but her marriage had recently broken up, and she returned to Louisville seeking support from her family.

Barry Sr., who owned a majority of the business, put his two daughters on the board of directors. They were delighted, although it appears that Sallie was also somewhat disappointed at not being asked to take a management job at the newspaper. Her feelings grew, although conflicts did not really get discussed by the family or at board meetings. The family had a long history of not being able to disagree or express conflict. However, Barry Jr. knew about their dissatisfaction, because both his mother and Sallie wrote letters to the editor disagreeing with political stands the paper took. Evidently Sallie was upset that the business did not offer daughters the same job opportunities as sons, and expressed these feelings as political disagreements in the letters.

In 1983 the conflict came into the open. Barry Jr. asked his father to request that Sallie and Eleanor resign from the board. Sallie refused. Then she demanded that the family buy out her shares of stock or she would sell them to an outsider. Increasingly Barry Jr. felt his family had lost faith in his management, although they never told him directly. He tried to work out several arrangements with Sallie and with Eleanor, who wanted to trade her stock for ownership of the TV station so she could run that. The major battle was over the value of Sallie's stock, and how much the company would pay to buy her shares. Barry Jr. stood firm in offering her a lower price than she wanted, and the two were unable to compromise.

Never expressing it openly, Barry Sr. felt deeply torn, and didn't know what to do. Although close with his wife, he wasn't able to bring his son and daughter together to look at the issues. He told the pair that if they couldn't come to an agreement he would sell the papers, but he was never active in getting the two to talk. In the conflict, Sallie cut off contact with her mother, and then with her father. This hurt Barry Sr. Suddenly, without discussing it with anyone but Mary, he announced that he had decided to sell the entire business to Gannett. Barry Jr. felt betrayed.

Everybody made a lot of money in the sale, but nobody was happy. The parents were estranged from their children, and the sons from the daughters. The family name was taken from the newspapers, where they had a proud tradition of liberal political and community involvement, and the wounds are so great that it is unlikely, particularly with Barry Sr.'s recent death, that the family can ever feel comfortable together again. Yet the sale was made to resolve a conflict.

What went wrong? Barry Jr. and Sallie each blame the other, while it is clear that either party could have forged a compromise. But by the end, neither one felt they could "give in," even when the sale was announced. Observers regret that Barry Sr. never got Sallie and Barry together to resolve their issues, and never asked them to reflect on the family tradition of service. To reach a compromise, Barry Sr. also might have gotten together with his children individually, trying to listen and discover what each really wanted.

The Binghams faced a classic family business conflict: the different perspectives, needs, and rights of passive owners in a family business, as opposed to the family members who run the businesses. And they transferred family difficulty and sibling rivalry (who was listened to, who was respected by Dad, who had more power) into a struggle over the future of the business. Both the business and the family lost.

It appears that the whole tragedy came about because the family didn't have a way to get people to sit down and talk about family issues. Instead feelings got played out in stock valuation, in newspaper columns, and in board meetings. The principals never got together over a dinner table, or in their homes, to explore the deep feelings of rivalry between Barry and Sallie. Clearly Sallie never felt recognized by her parents and Barry Jr. never felt supported by them. By the close of the drama, each person was willing to lose everything rather than compromise. Such is the case in most family feuds. In a feud, people are more concerned that the other person not get something, rather than trying to get what they want.

It would appear that Binghams never learned to communicate or to face conflict. This is not an uncommon problem. Often families avoid or deny conflict, until it erupts into painful and sometimes unresolvable schisms. This deficiency can cripple or even destroy a family business because conflict is a reality of business life. The Binghams and many others had to sell their businesses because they did not know how to talk about their feelings, hurts, differences, and change. But by learning clear and direct family communication and conflict resolution, you can avoid such pitfalls.

Tasks for the Chapter

In this chapter, you will learn how to talk with the members of your family business who create the most difficulty and distress for you. You will learn some techniques for getting behind the problem, for clarifying issues, and for understanding what is "really" going on. You'll find ways to get the attention of family members who are not eager to talk about something, and how to separate the "family" from the "business" aspect of conflicts. You will learn how to hold problem-solving meetings with particular family members to discuss difficult issues before they become "family feuds."

Many techniques and examples of family communication difficulties will be presented. There are exercises for family members who do not feel heard, for people who are feeling anger or hurt, for people who want to reconsider family or business traditions, and for those who wish to

*resolve value and policy differences. Special focus will be on communi-
cating with people who "won't listen." While the exercises focus on
communication between family members, they are equally applicable to
difficulties between outside managers and family members.*

Why is Communication So Difficult?

From the outside, it seems so easy to resolve many of the difficulties
of families in business. Yet many families will stop at nothing to avoid
discussion of controversial issues. Why are communication and conflict
resolution so especially difficult for family business?

The reason is that in a family business, you can't just have a talk about
business differences. Family members do not merely face differences of
opinion, feelings, or conflicts over policies. They bring with them not
just the issue at hand, but a history of expectations, assumptions, hurts,
and unfulfilled desires as ghosts in the conversation. For example in a
business setting when a CEO father asks his accountant daughter to get
him a cup of coffee, he is not just making a simple request. He is also
sending a signal about the terms of the relationship and their history. He
assumes that he has the right to ask her and that she will obey. But what
if she were to reply, "No Dad, why don't you ask one of the other vice-
presidents?," or "That's a job for your secretary"? Then they would be
arguing over the rules of their relationship. She would be calling upon the
assumptions of a work relationship, while he assumes the family relationship is still in effect. You can imagine the arguments at home and over
lunch that might ensue, and how other family members—his wife, his
son, and his other daughter—might take sides! Often in order to avoid
conflict, women who find themselves in this situation choose to say
nothing, but their resentment builds and may come out in covert ways.

Now consider that this same daughter wants her father to consider a
new form of accounting, or that a brother-in-law is arguing with the boss'
son about responsibility. In each case they are struggling not just with the
issue, but with their history together, and the nature of their relationship.
Resolving conflicts in family business means not just finding good com-
promises to deep business or personal issues, but understanding that
every family conversation deals with the reality of the family and
business history. All the baggage family relationships carry gets in the
way of sharing and resolving differences. It would be great if when
children or other family members come to work, they could start their
relationship with family members afresh. But this just can't happen.

Reflection Question

Think about your work relationships with family members, especially the ones you disagree with or fight with. For each person, ask yourself what expectations, needs, assumptions, habits, or frustrations you carry into the current relationship from your family history together. You might have a talk with the other person and ask him or her what he or she brings from the past.

Sources of Conflict

Despite the rich variety of conflicts and communication difficulties that arise in family business, there are actually a very few issues that create them. As you can see, they are all interrelated and cluster around the dual relationship of family member and business associate. Knowing about these common issues can help you identify what is going on in your family business when there's a problem. If you are having a family conflict, you should go through this list and ask yourself whether some of these feelings lie below the surface.

1. Violation of one's sense of fairness or justice.

Everybody grows up with a sense of what is fair and to be expected from the business and the family. Such common assumptions as "every child gets treated equally" are articles of faith. But often these can be interpreted differently. But equal treatment, particularly in a business setting, becomes a problem due to different talents, activities, and circumstances.

For instance a family that wants to treat children equally has a problem when one child is running the business in such a way that its profits increase manyfold. As a key manager, he or she has a right to ask for a hefty share of the profits, but as a child in the family, his or her share may have been determined at birth. In addition, the brother who is a doctor may see the whole situation differently from his home three states away, and spouses may have their own perspectives. Father and Mother, of course, have their own views: they may need income for their retirement so they want to reward the child who is succeeding, but they may also want all the kids to be happy and feel good about their inheritance. And the parents even may disagree with one another about what's fair. So even the simplest principle of the family can be sorely tested over the years.

What is fair and just extends to how you are treated when you are hurt. For example, Fred hired Joe, his contractor brother-in-law, to build an office for the family business. Fred felt the work was not done up to standards, but didn't feel he could confront Joe. So he kept quiet. When the time came to build a second office, he gave the contract to another builder, offending Joe. The sister/spouse felt caught in the middle. Who should talk to whom? Is Joe really aware that he disappointed Fred, and might he have put in the additional work if asked? Or will he get angry and defensive, and accuse Fred of presuming on their relationship to get extra work done? Should Fred apologize or change his behavior? What is fair in this situation? Many family conflicts in business stem from balancing family notions of fairness.

2. Feeling unacknowledged.

This problem arises in family business when you don't feel that your contribution, talent, or ability is noticed by others, especially parents. They may be critical, or they may ignore your achievements. Your parents may have trouble seeing you as grown, or seeing the value of your work. They may not reward your contribution with the kind of salary or job that fits your value, or they may give your older sibling more attention. This situation is very common in companies, where many non-family employees also feel unacknowledged. People in general are very reticent about noticing positive things that others do and we often go around feeling unappreciated or "ripped off."

The conflict becomes even more difficult in a family business, because you may not feel acknowledged or even loved as a person by your relative, and then transfer that personal feeling to the business. I once knew a young man who felt ignored and unappreciated by his father. He decided to work in the family business so his father finally would notice him. As his father continued to be negative and critical, over time the son gave up trying to do a good job.

3. Feeling powerless.

Closely related to feeling unappreciated, a sense of powerlessness arises when you feel you don't have any impact on other family members. They won't listen to your advice nor heed your ideas and judgments. This is a common problem caused by family roles. A family member can be a professional, with tremendous competency, but the family role of "Little Brother or Sister," or simply "Son or Daughter" can prevent that ability from being recognized. Often, for instance, when a sibling comes from working in another business to the family business, he or she can see certain problems in the business that Father or Older Brother find it difficult to acknowledge because the advice is coming from Younger Brother or Sister.

This situation often arises when you have outside professional experience or have performed well in the business, and your father cannot see you as anything but an irresponsible child. This makes some children work even harder, if fruitlessly, while it leads others to just give up. The challenge is to separate the real business issue, such as a needed shift of strategy, new product, or market pressure, from the family's emotional issue. The business suffers when a family role prevents the consideration of a business need.

4. Confusion of family and business roles.

Family members talk to each other without being aware of what role they are taking, and, as we saw in Chapter 2, often transfer family roles into the business. Remember the daughter/manager who was asked by her father/boss to get him coffee? That's a classic example of role confusion.

Myths about Conflict and Communication

Most family business conflicts are resolvable. However we are often limited in coming to a resolution by some common myths about conflict and communication, such as:

1. Since he or she won't change there is nothing I can do.

This attitude is probably the biggest roadblock to resolution. It puts the blame on the other person, rather than where it belongs—between you and the other person. By giving up before you start, you lose any chance to try new ways to resolve the problem. By focussing on the other person, you lose the possibility of modifying your own choices in the situation. Conflict resolution begins with you. What can *you* do to create a positive climate for the other person to work on the problem?

2. He or she just doesn't care or doesn't want to do anything.

You usually think this when someone is not doing what you want. It assumes the other person knows your wants and needs, which he or she usually doesn't. Before assuming the other person's disinterest in you, you might try to air your concerns more clearly and ask the other person where he or she stands. Rather than make assumptions, talk to the other person about yourself and about what he or she wants, feels, and needs.

3. Conflict is bad and wrong if people love each other.

This is a very common myth. But the truth is we don't always agree with people we love, and, in fact, we don't usually have conflicts with people we don't care about. Many families attempt to avoid conflict at all costs, or assume that there is something wrong if two people disagree. They believe that if they talk about a problem, it will get worse, or out of control, or hurt somebody. Yet, if you don't acknowledge a conflict, it doesn't go away. It just remains below the surface, building up. When it finally explodes, it is usually worse for having been avoided for so long. Then everybody's worst fears come true.

4. Feelings have no place in business relationships.

You'd be surprised how many people think this. Actually, of course, all relationships are about feelings of love, caring, and respect. In addition, every family business conflict has an emotional component that must be addressed along with the practical issue at stake. People in families are not rational beings, and they need leeway to discuss the emotional side of issues, such as wanting to be accepted, or feeling hurt or ignored. Every family relationship can generate tremendous feelings. While feelings can be put aside when decisions are made, they need to be acknowledged first.

Self Defeating Responses to Conflict

Family business disagreements often grow out of proportion due to ineffective and counterproductive responses by family members. We are usually raised with a very small repertoire of problem-solving methods, and don't know what to do when these methods fail. Conflict management theorists Jordan and Margaret Paul, in a workbook on family conflict resolution[1], observe that family members tend to respond to disagreements in three typical but self-defeating, non-productive ways. Assuming erroneously that they can't deal directly with the other person, they either try to control or coerce the other, withdraw into apathy or defeat, or try to manipulate indirectly. None of these strategies really brings about a resolution.

Strategy One: Controlling or Coercing the Other.

Using threats, withdrawal of emotional support, and other punishments, some family members try to force the others to do what they want. For example, one son stopped talking to his mother when he had a business dispute with his father. Another brother threatened to quit or sue.

Many parents routinely talk about disinheriting their children if they do not do as they wish. Often they have no real intention to follow through, which hurts their credibility. When people feel there's no other way to get what they want, they may resort to threats.

Often value differences become control issues, leading to fruitless conflict, because the real issues are not brought to the surface. Many parents want to help their children by controlling their decisions. It is hard for parents to see a child, even an adult child, make a decision they feel will be "harmful." Other family members go along without really wanting to. Their feelings build up. The child ends up feeling controlled and coerced, and may undermine or rebel.

When a business is involved, the parental pressure may be to make a career choice to enter the business, or to do something else that the family values. Parents always find it hard to let go of expectations of their children. This reality came to me personally. I had been working with a family business where the parents were very controlling of their children, from picking their schools, to getting them jobs in banks. I came home and my teen-age son Oren, who goes to a school that requires community service, excitedly told me that he had found the perfect place to do his service work: working with a community group to build a downtown ballpark in San Francisco! Now Oren comes from a long-line of community activists and socially responsible family members, and, for whatever reasons, this was not our idea of what the community most needed. There were talks between his parents and our contemporaries about what to do, automatically taking the form "Should we let him do it?" Our initial response, like those of many other parents, was to pressure him to do what we felt was right. Ultimately, we simply decided to let him know that we respected his decision, but it certainly wasn't the decision any of us would have made. He changed his mind. I learned from this how easily parents' sense of what is good for their children can shift into coercion or pressure.

Our culture is very supportive of coercion, threats, and bluster. Unfortunately, when you force someone to do something, you often get their agreement at the cost of the relationship. People feel more estranged, less trusting, and less willing to share information when they are coerced. In families, anger at coercive tactics can lead over time to feuds or total breaks of relationships.

Strategy Two: Withdrawing into Apathy.

Giving up diminishes your self-esteem, and is an admission that you have no influence over the other person or the situation. Both assumptions are wrong, and have drastic consequences. They lead you to lose positive energy and commitment, often over a relationship or business that means a great deal to you. This stance is a dead end—there is nowhere you can go from here.

Feeling defeated is different from strategic withdrawal or making a positive decision to let go. The question is whether you move on to another focus of interest and seek out other opportunities, or keep feeling upset, hurt, or limited by a situation where you didn't get what you want. Are you able to let go, or are you consumed by bitterness?

Strategy Three: Manipulating Indirectly.

Early in life, when they can't reach their goals or get what they want from siblings or parents, children learn to do it indirectly. The child who goes to the other parent to ask for money, the son who, after being told no, sneaks out and does what he wants anyway, or the wife who gets sick to avoid a social engagement are all getting what they want indirectly.

Indeed many self-help tomes and business bibles are manuals of how to manipulate people to get what you want subversively. This may be helpful in more distant business dealings, but when you try to get people close to you to do things indirectly, you lose some important things. First, the issue cannot be talked about openly. Second, communication about what you really want isn't taking place. And finally, you are not treating the other person with respect and honesty. All of these costs are intangible, while the immediate benefit of manipulation may be experienced today. However, like the other strategies, manipulation caries more costs than benefits as a long-term way of managing family/business relationships.

Redesigning Relationships for Communication

Whenever I talk to family business members, they almost uniformly report their most pressing concern is "communication." What they usually mean is that they have trouble getting another family member to do what they want. They want to "communicate" to the other why he or she should do something. More often than not, the concern for communication is really about control. The story of family business and indeed of many families is about the efforts of some members to get the others to do something. Parents want their children to behave in a certain way, and children, especially when they follow parents into their business, want to have impact on parents. Often they have different ideas about what to do, but, unfortunately, only a single business to operate.

In general, people want to force others to change as a last resort. In most situations, they really want the other person to sit down and listen. Only after they don't feel heard and respected do they get into battles over control and lose the possibility of compromise.

The primary communication issue in family businesses is the difficulty family members—spouses, parents, children, siblings—have really hearing one other. They have been together so long that they often stop listening, thinking they "know" the other. But effective communication is about really listening to the other members of your family and allowing them to remain different, even respecting their differences.

Problems in communication can't be resolved in a five-minute chat or even with a formal, "Let's sit down and work this out." Often communication problems have built up over a long time, and they are usually broader than just resolving one difference. Communication is not just applying a series of techniques to a conversation, but implies a set of attitudes about the other person and the relationship. Good communication means a good relationship. A good relationship is one where people

• Have basic respect for each other;
• Take time to listen to and learn about each other;
• Allow each other to be different;
• Consider preserving the relationship to be more important
  than any particular issue.

When a relationship contains these elements, there is no dispute that cannot be resolved. Without the above elements, it is unlikely that even minor differences can be bridged. While it can't be measured or seen, the most important thing to bring to improving a relationship is the attitude that the relationship, and the other person, is important to you.

People often look at this list and say, "Well, I act that way with **him**, but he doesn't reciprocate." That attitude is self-defeating, and leaves you waiting for the other to improve the relationship. The other person would probably say the same thing about you! To redesign a relationship for good communication, you need to begin with yourself. You help create the environment for the other person, and there are more ways to change that environment than you probably have considered. A person who appears to "resist" open communication can be drawn out, involved, or persuaded to open up under the right conditions.

The place to begin to build communication is with yourself. First you need to conduct a self-exploration of what you want to achieve through communication, and then you have to do a critical analysis of your strategies. Many of us spend a lot of time and energy thinking about how we wish the other person would be, rather than on what we want, or what we may be doing to keep the other person from talking to us.

For example, a son wanted to know more about his father's incredible ability to make financial deals. He felt cut out, as if his father didn't trust him enough to teach him. He kept demanding to be included and even got angry at his father, arguing with him about business policy. But when the son stopped focusing on what his father was doing and looked at his own behavior, he saw that he was afraid of not measuring up to his dad's ability. So he created situations for his father to exclude him, and picked self-defeating arguments. A change was able to occur when he let his father know that he felt distrusted and that he greatly valued his father's expertise. Previously his father had seen him as a know-it-all, not willing to listen. The father never felt valued or appreciated by his son.

Like so many communication cutoffs, in this one each person felt the other did not value him. When the truth was communicated, the situation got much better. Here the key was that the son looked first to changing his own behavior to improve the situation.

The second step to improving communication with a family member is to know the other person better. You can't resolve a conflict without knowing the other person. So if your son, daughter, or brother-in-law is the difficult person in your family business for you, you need to specifically work on that relationship, not avoid it. Put aside the issue at hand, what you want from the other, and try to focus on learning about the person as someone you care about and appreciate. Often when you learn more about someone you can understand why he or she is stubborn about a certain issue.

For example, many business founders seem closed to new ideas, set in their ways, and unwilling to compromise with their raring-to-go heirs entering the business. One son couldn't understand why his parents, who founded a retail store 20 years before, weren't willing to invest in advertising, open a new store, or initiate an inventory control system. He felt angry and superior to their small-business mentality. They dug in. Then he began to listen to them. He heard stories he had heard before, but never really listened to, about their childhood poverty, their feelings about debt, and their concerns about cash for retirement. He understood that they didn't want to lose what they had or forfeit control of their business. They needed security, while he needed challenge and risk. The solution to this conflict was simple: working with his own advisors, he offered to buy the business from his parents at extremely generous terms that included their managing the flagship store for another five years. Once he heard what was really at stake, he could provide what they both needed.

Seek out the person. Let him or her know that you want to improve your relationship. But then tell the person that since the conflict seems so difficult to each of you, you first just want to spend some time together. Have dinner, spend an evening or a day. Your goal is to talk about what really is important to you, and for each of you to get to know the other better, to develop the trust and understanding which are necessary for real conflict resolution. Sometimes I've seen people begin to work better together just because they feel closer, even though they never really resolved their "issue." As they learn to value the relationship as a whole, the problem becomes less important.

A case in point: a brother and brother-in-law had several angry confrontations. Then an opportunity came for the two of them to take a trip to work with a factory that was in grave crisis. Spending two days together, and working closely together, increased their appreciation of one another's skills and commitment to the business. When they came back to their core issues two weeks later, there was a significant shift in how they felt. They had affirmed their relationship, and they saw that each was deeply committed to the success of the company.

In your conversations, focus especially on your shared and different family histories. If the person comes from another family or another part of your family, try to understand their perspective before you share yours. For instance, Jim felt that his brother-in-law, Will, was after his job. But then they spent some time together and Jim learned that his brother-in-law was in the middle of a family of five very competitive boys. No wonder he had to fight to assert himself! This awareness allowed Jim to see that what he took as a personal attack was just Will's style of survival.

You should be open to learning about yourself, reconsidering your positions, and getting a new perspective on your conflict. If you are willing to step back from your position, your example may have the same effect on your antagonist.

One key quality of effective dialogue is persistence. It takes time for one person to change, and by persisting in your desire to work on the relationship, you can keep the process going. I am continually amazed how family members talk about how important something is to them, but then give up after a few minutes of conversation. Persevere!

You also want to look at all the areas you agree on. A conflict becomes less critical when you and another person discover you agree on 90%. You should share your basic assumptions about the business, and talk about what you want from it. You should talk about what you want from the business, and from your relationship.

You also need to look closely at what you want to get from the other person. Your initial response will probably be that you want the person to stop doing the thing that upset you or to do something you want done. How is that likely to happen? Let's say you're upset about your father putting you down. You may threaten him by saying, "If you put me down again, I'll quit." Or you may do to him what he did to you, putting him down for putting you down. What's wrong with these aggressive responses is that they do not have the total result you want. Looking behind your feelings, you probably want more than for him to stop due to your pressure. Rather you want him to stop or change because he really understands how his behavior has affected you. It is sometimes more important to have the other person understand how you feel than to have a behavior change.

Exercise: It May Not Be All His or Her Problem

Consider a person in your family business with whom you have difficulty communicating, or with whom you would like to have a more open relationship. Begin by looking at yourself in this relationship. Take time to consider, and write your responses, to the following:

1. *What do I want from this other person?*
2. *What is the particular issue between us?*
3. *What conflicts have we had, and what has happened to them?*
4. *What issues, topics, or feelings do we avoid discussing?*
5. *What do I feel that this other person does not understand about me?*
6. *What do I most appreciate and value about the other person?*
7. *What am I most afraid will happen if I really let the other person know what I feel?*
8. *What issues are at stake or lie behind the issue we differ on? (These can be family history, old feelings, or things that you want from the other that may not directly apply to the current issue.)*
9. *What would I be willing to give up in order to have a deeper relationship with this other person? Be specific.*
10. *What do I do when I talk to this person that may make him or her less willing to communicate with me? How do I turn off or tune out?*
11. *Am I really willing to listen to what the other person has to say, rather than just wanting him or her to do what I want? What makes it difficult for me to listen to the other person?*

Don't set them up for failure.

Sam Steinberg (A) and (B) (Condensed)

In 1969, Sam Steinberg was 64 years old. He had been running the family business, Steinberg's, for over 50 years. The business had grown from a single storefront in the heart of Montreal's Jewish community to a chain of over 170 grocery stores with 17,500 employees, nearly half a billion dollars in sales, and profits of over $6 million.

In March of 1969, Sam Steinberg convened a meeting of the company's senior executives to discuss the future of the business and to solicit input on the choice of successor. Sam had decided, with some prodding from his board, to step up to the newly created post of chairman and to appoint a successor to the presidency.

Background

Sam Steinberg was born in eastern Hungary in 1905. His mother, Ida Roth, had been born nearby in 1884. (See **Exhibit 1** for family genealogy.) She had married Vilmos Sternberg in 1902 when she was 18 and Vilmos was 27. The marriage was typical for the period—Ida met Vilmos the day before the wedding. Two years after the marriage, a son, Jack, was born and a year later, in 1905, Sam arrived. (Clark, 16-17)

Vilmos was a baker but not a steady worker, preferring to spend his time at prayer at the Synagogue. Ida took up baking herself and brought her goods to the market each day. In this way she supported her growing family. (Clark, 17)

A note on sources: Several published sources of material proved invaluable in compiling this case series on Sam Steinberg, including:

-   *Steinberg: . . . a Family Empire*, by Ann Gibbon and Peter Hadekel. (Ontario: MacMillan of Canada, 1990)
-   *We Grew Like Topsy*, by Henry Mintzberg and James A. Waters. (Montreal: McGill University, Unpublished paper, 1979)
-   *For Good Measure*, by Gerald Clark. (Toronto: McClelland and Stewart, 1986, private edition)

The reader should assume when a source is noted at the end of a paragraph that the material in that entire paragraph is based upon the source noted.

Professor Michael J. Roberts prepared this case with the assistance of Anthony G. Athos and Nan-b and Philippe de Gaspé Beaubien of the International Centre for Family Enterprises as the basis for class discussion rather than to illustrate either effective or ineffective handling of an administrative situation. This case was condensed from the Sam Steinberg (A) and the Sam Steinberg (B) cases (HBS Nos. 392-059 and 392-060).

1

Another son, Nathan, was born in 1907; a daughter, Lily, was born in 1909. In 1911, at the urging of her three sisters already in Montreal, Ida and Vilmos brought their family over to live in Montreal (where, during the immigration process, Sternberg was accidently changed to Steinberg). The Steinberg family lived in a house with Ida's sisters. In 1912 Max was born, and in 1914, Morris. The Steinbergs had many mouths to feed, and Ida put her children to work hawking newspapers, spotting pins in the bowling alley, and doing odd jobs to help support the family. (Clark, 18-20)

A book on Sam Steinberg, *For Good Measure*, described the part of Montreal where Sam was raised:

They [the Jewish immigrants] settled in a kind of ribbon, one block east and one block west of the Main, and they hung around the street corners; that was where bosses and foremen picked up pressers or buttonhole makers as they needed them.

Maybe half of the people had the skills or luck to find such work. The rest drifted into some sort of selling—as pedlars or in shops of their own. These were tiny establishments—groceries, candy stores, hardware, dry goods—that required virtually no capital. There was no such thing as credit rating; the banks wouldn't lend, anyway, to unknowns. (Clark, 15-16)

According to *Steinberg*, Vilmos never quite adapted to life in Canada, preferring to spend his time engaged in odd jobs and as a sexton at the local synagogue. And, shortly after the Steinberg's had settled, he and Ida split up. Ida's sisters talked her into leaving Vilmos; the Steinberg family could simply not afford to have any more children. (Gibbon & Hadekel, 39)

Steinberg's: The Beginning

With Vilmos gone, Ida had to look for more opportunities to earn money for her family. In 1917 she found a small storefront on St. Lawrence Boulevard, the "Main Street" of the Montreal Jewish community. There, with an investment of between $200 and $500, she opened a small grocery store. Like most of the other grocery stores of the time, it was a full-service operation: orders were taken, filled, and delivered. Ida displayed a talent for arranging and displaying the wares and for excellent service. The shop soon had a loyal following among the immigrant poor who were always searching for the best prices. (Gibbon & Hadekel, 41)

The nine members of the extended family—Ida, her six children and two sisters—lived in a small apartment above the store. *For Good Measure* described the family's living arrangements:

It was only about twenty feet wide, but fairly deep. The back was converted into a kitchen and dining room, occupied more by cartons and crates than by furniture. . . . Upstairs, in what had once been a clothing factory, were the bedrooms Whoever of the boys got out of bed first was able to grab the least-frayed shirt. There was cold running water and an indoor toilet, but no bathtub. (Clark, 23)

According to *Steinberg*, Ida instilled a powerful set of values in her children, all of whom worked and had specific jobs at the store. Sam became the store buyer, and Nathan was his assistant. Jack made deliveries, and Lily took orders. In addition to their work at the store, the Steinberg boys also sold newspapers and performed odd jobs—anything to supplement the family's income. (Gibbon & Hadekel, 44)

Steinberg suggests that Sam soon outshone his siblings in the talent he displayed for the business. He became the undisputed leader of the family and its business. By the time he was 14, he

2

had stopped attending school and was working at the grocery full time. While Sam relished the responsibility and the opportunity to oblige his mother, he occasionally complained when he was working and his other brothers were off playing. (Gibbon & Hadekel, 46) His mother would answer him, "If you've got two horses hitched to your cart, a spirited one and a lazy one, whip up the spirited one and other will follow along." (Clark, 27)

Soon Sam began to make most of the key decisions. When he was 13, he rented the space next door to the store so that they could expand operations. Shortly thereafter, he purchased another piece of property across town and opened a second store. Sam recalled the events:

> A little guy by the name of Israelovitch...came to sell me rice. . . . One day he comes to see me when I was trimming celery in the back of the store, that there is a store for sale on Bernard Avenue, so I went up to see it...I said to him what does he want for the store. Well he wanted $1,000. What did he have in the store, I counted it quick like lightening, I added up his groceries—$600 worth of groceries, he had the shelving, he had the counter, he had a scale, cash register, coffee grinder, and a meat slicer. That was his equipment. And an ice box. He wanted $1,000. So I said OK, I'd buy it. (Mintzberg & Waters, 91)

Sam's mother came up with the $2,000 it took to buy and stock the store. She embraced the opportunity to install Nathan as manager of this operation, repeatedly emphasizing that the family's welfare had to be the top priority. "Sam, you must look after the boys," she said. (Mintzberg & Waters, 48) Nathan also recalled his mother's words in those years as she saw a competitor's delivery cart go by: "Some day we'll have horses like that." (Mintzberg & Waters, 91) *Steinberg* reports that there was only one qualification you needed to handle the cash in the store: "You had to be family." (Gibbon & Hadekel, 45)

Sam took on the responsibility for managing the stores. He recalled those early years:

> I wanted to go to school, but my mother needed somebody in the store. I had an older brother, Jack, but she didn't feel that he was suited for the store, and she wanted me to stop school. So, you know, like all the kids you like to play, and school was play, and the store was work. So I felt very bad about it, and I made up my mind. The first year that I was working, and how I remember, I was delivering a message, walking along the Marie-Anne. The first store I saw was at the corner of Clark and Marie-Anne...little bit of a store, size of this room [he points around his office, on the top floor of the Alexis Nihon Plaza], the whole store...if it was as big as this room. Dark, dingy, with a husband and wife working, you know. And I question myself—how long they were in business—and I think I found out 10 years. Goddamit, after 10 years in business, I'm not going to look like that. You see, that's where you...right there and then. I made up my mind. (Mintzberg & Waters, 92)

In 1928 Sam, then 22, married Helen Roth, his first cousin. With the marriage Sam acquired more obligations. He formed a partnership with Helen's father (Lewis Roth) and turned the Roth's fruit store into a Steinberg's. With his brother running one store and his father-in law another, there were still plenty of Steinbergs who needed to be supported. (Clark, 34)

Sam recalled the pressures that led to expansion:

> I just was meeting the needs. My brother was in this store, my father-in-law with his children was in the Outremont Fruit Store. Now that's too much of a load in terms of family for these stores to support. It was common sense. So I looked for another store...I started thinking, when they get married how are they going to live, I even started thinking about that when I was a little boy in the Main Street... It was

always a concern of necessity, it was a question of survival, it was a question of not permitting outside change to take away our livelihood, that was the challenge. (Mintzberg & Waters, 92-93)

Arnold Steinberg, Sam's nephew, explained how Sam acquired control of the company that was to become Steinberg's:

> Sam formed a company with his mother's brother—his father-in-law—Lewis Roth. They each had half. Then Lewis Roth's wife died, and he went back to Hungary and married his former wife's sister. Lewis gave most of his stock to his four children, including Sam's wife, Helen. He kept a small piece for himself. Sam then had his wife's stock, and then he got another 12.5% when he bought out his oldest brother-in-law, who was uncomfortable working for Sam. Sam paid $7,000 for his stock. As Sam continued to open stores, he put his brothers in charge of them, and they received stock over the years. But Sam was always careful to keep at least 51% under his control.

By 1930, there were three stores. Sam Roth and Lawrence Roth, (who were simultaneously Sam's cousins and brothers-in-law) each ran a store. Sam ran a store with his brother Nathan. In addition, Sam functioned as president; Jack was in charge of maintenance; Nathan, fruit buying; Max, construction; and Sam Cohen, a cousin, grocery buying. (Mintzberg & Waters, 56)

Expansion

In 1931, Sam opened three new stores, doubling the size of the small chain. Although the depression was still casting its shadow over business in Montreal, it created an opportunity for Steinberg's. Chains—such as Dominion and A & P—were closing stores, and Steinberg's was picking up the slack. (Mintzberg & Waters, 95)

Jack Levine recalled the early years at Steinberg's:

> Sam was running a store and doing the buying and administration at the same time. When it got to be five or six stores, he bumped himself up from the store and began managing the overall company.

At the same time, a new mode of grocery retailing was taking hold—self-service. Sam visited Loblaw's, a Canadian chain in Toronto, to see how they were implementing the concept. He was impressed and by 1934 had opened a self-service store in Montreal under the name "Wholesale Groceteria," so as not to confuse "Steinberg's" customers. Sam slashed prices 15%-20% below what they were in the full service operation, and customers flocked to the store. Sam retold the history of how the change came about:

> So let me tell you this, because this is crucial; this has been the history of Steinberg's: I opened the store, it wasn't doing business, went through one summer. So what did I do? Over one weekend...I said this is no good; we ripped off the Steinberg's sign, put on Wholesale Groceteria—not Steinberg, but Wholesale Groceteria—reduced all the prices, got a gang from the office, reduced the prices, very sharp, sent out a circular...we opened it as a Wholesale Groceteria and it was so busy you couldn't get into the store. (Mintzberg & Waters, 95)

Sam had also come to realize that with expansion and the need to hire non-family employees, Steinberg's commitment to personal service would be difficult to maintain.

4

Loblaw's were self-service even when I was on the Main street... I believe in [personal] service because I knew Mrs. Mintzberg or Mrs. Circus or anybody, I knew what she would like; I'd tell her what to buy, you know. How could they compete with all that knowledge, self-service, what would the customer know? So I went down to see it [in Ottawa]. And I saw the people how they shopped in self- service... You know what I came to realize? That I was judging all my employees by myself. That because I knew, didn't mean my clerks knew; in fact, I found out when I thought of it they did more harm than good. (Mintzberg & Waters, 96)

A second Wholesale Groceteria was opened soon after. This was Store Number 8, where Jack Levine was the manager—the first non-family member to run a store. With the success of the second store, Sam knew he was on to something: "... when we had learned how to operate that," Sam Steinberg continued, "it became a way of life. Then we knew we were on our way. . . . I came home and told my wife, 'boy, we've got it made.'" (Mintzberg & Waters, 97) By 1935, all of Steinberg's had been converted to Groceterias, and Sam was running 11 stores.

Sam made frequent innovations, always scouring the market for the latest ideas and inventing many himself. Sam saw shopping carts used for the first time in the U.S. and brought the idea to Canada. He boosted sales of produce by wrapping fruits and vegetables in clear plastic wrap—then an innovation. (Gibbon & Hadekel, 52)

By 1939 there were 23 Steinberg's stores, all self-service Wholesale Groceterias. Steinberg's executives trace the evolution of the supermarket from this year—1939—when meat was first available in the store. Self-service in the fruit and vegetable departments was introduced the following year, and the meat department went self-service in 1943—the first in North America to do so. (Mintzberg & Waters, 25)

The rise of the supermarket changed the economics of the grocery retailing business in dramatic fashion (see **Exhibit 2**). The average capital investment for a chain store in 1930 (e.g., A&P) was $5,062, and sales averaged $67,000. The supermarket concept increased the capital required to something over $30,000, but sales could be increased by an even greater multiple. (Tedlow, 230)

The advent of war brought growth to a standstill, as many grocery products were rationed and/or price controlled. Steinberg's had 30 stores in 1942, and 31 in 1947. Still, Sam managed to cement Steinberg's place in the market with his ethical, customer-oriented approach to business. While many other grocers would divert scarce goods and sell them privately for sums far higher than the official price, Steinberg's continued to offer low prices and a good selection of whatever goods it could get its hands on. Customers became more loyal than ever. In addition, Steinberg's was able to perfect many of the practices of the modern supermarket, which had still been quite new at the start of the decade. (Mintzberg & Waters, 105)

Post-War Growth

The one benefit of the war period was that Steinberg's had been able to use its cash reserves to acquire land at attractive prices. The same migration to the suburbs that was occurring in the U.S. was under way in Canada, and Steinberg's was positioned to cash in on the trend. The company had begun to introduce private-label products during the 1930s, and this trend accelerated. In 1946 the company began manufacturing its own grocery products. It roasted its own coffee and nuts and began producing its own tea bags. Bakery production began in the same year, and Steinberg's baked its own products for its stores and others. (Mintzberg & Waters, 107)

This growth forced a certain articulation of the company's structure. Sam was still involved in all dimensions of the business, but a simple functional structure had evolved. (Mintzberg & Waters, 57)

By the early 1950s, Sam Steinberg was able to see the huge growth in the supermarket business that would be engendered by the shifting populace. As the company began to expand, Sam realized that he could not afford to rely on the whim of developers to let him in to the shopping centers that were then being built. According to Arnold Steinberg, Sam said that "we can't be at the mercy of those guys; we'll only get every third or fourth store; we have to go into it." So Steinberg's decided it needed to be in the shopping center development business. (Mintzberg & Waters, 114)

The company needed funds to finance this expansion, and Sam finally found a securities firm that would raise money for Steinberg's without requiring the family to give up ownership. In 1952, Steinberg's sold $5 million of general debentures, announcing that the money would be used to build 25 new stores over the next five years. And in 1955, the company raised another $5 million via an issue of preferred stock. (Mintzberg & Waters, 114-115)

In addition, Steinberg's was investing in its warehouse and bakery capacity during the period of the late 1950s. This, in addition to the continuing demand for money to fund expansion, led to the decision to go public. In 1957, the company sold 500,000 shares of non-voting, Class A common stock for $17 each, raising $8.5 million. (Mintzberg & Waters, 116-120) The shares were soon trading at $25. (*Business Week*, 116) When the company went public, the board consisted of Sam, his brothers Nathan and Max, and cousin/brother-in-law Sam Roth. The first non-family director was added to the board in this year. By 1959, the board had been expanded to include (in addition to the above) Sam's other two brothers, two additional cousins, Steinberg's executive Jack Genzer, and Sam's personal attorney Lazarus Phillips. (Mintzberg & Waters, 122)

Between 1953 and 1960, the company added stores at an average of one every 47 days. And the bulk of this growth came through the focus on shopping centers. By 1960, 50 stores—41% of the total—were in shopping centers. This period also saw Steinberg's expand outside Montreal. In 1953, only 3 of 38 stores were outside Montreal. By 1958, the ratio was over 50%. (Mintzberg & Waters, 119)

Throughout, Sam focused on serving the customer. Certain stories circulated at Steinberg's to prove the point. One had Sam out driving when he saw a woman trudging home, laden down with Steinberg's bags. Sam offered to drive her home. Store managers learned quickly to go the extra mile, to do almost anything to please a customer. (Gibbon & Hadekel, 91)

One key to the success of Steinberg's strategy was its market research. The company performed extensive research on population trends, customer needs, and suppliers. A *Business Week* article on Steinberg's described some of their efforts:

> In effect, Steinberg's throws open its stores to manufacturers as practical laboratories. "In one case," says research head, Harry Suffrin, "we worked with a manufacturer for a whole year to help him measure the impact of his new line. We tried everything he wanted: aisle display, first-in-traffic flow, top shelf, middle shelf, the works. . . ."

> Suffrin uses 20 stores as his field lab—10 as controls where shelf space is frozen and no innovations are made. In the others, under close watch, experimentation gets free play. . . .

6

46

Steinberg's also has a 650-woman consumer panel that tests products continually to "help our male buyers see the women's side of the story." (*Business Week*, 119)

Continuing Growth and Diversification

In June of 1959, Steinberg's made its largest expansion move ever with the purchase of 39 Grand Union stores in the province of Ontario. (Mintzberg & Waters, 123) Just a few months earlier, in the January 1959 *Business Week* article, a Steinberg's executive had stated: "The day Loblaw moves into Quebec, that's the day we'll be in Ontario." A few weeks after that statement was made, it became known that Loblaw's had purchased a chain with 12 Montreal stores.

The initial results were not positive. One senior executive was quoted: "I don't think anyone visited the 39 stores." Another described it as "a lot of crummy locations." (Mintzberg & Waters, 129)

Loblaw's and Dominion, the two large chains in Ontario, reacted with widespread price promotions, and a prolonged price war ensued. Where Sam had an intimate knowledge of Montreal and could move quickly there, he knew little of Ontario. One executive described the situation: "It would take 23 trips and guys swearing their life on it to buy a site. . . . Without senior management there, Ontario was treated like a branch plant operation." (Mintzberg & Waters, 129-130)

In 1962, Steinberg's made its first expansion outside the grocery business: the Miracle Mart Discount Department Store. Sam perceived the existence of large general merchandisers who sold food as a loss leader as a threat to his core business. He also saw the discount department store as a way to apply his merchandising methods to a new line of goods. The business got off to a good start, but problems quickly developed. Steinberg's had no experience in the fashion business, and this was important with softgoods. Gradually, executives came to see the business as dramatically different from Steinberg's core grocery business, and its performance was a drag on earnings for many years. (Mintzberg & Waters, 141-144)

The company also took steps toward vertically integrating in its baking businesses. In 1966, the company invested in a new company—Cartier Refined Sugars—and purchased it in its entirety in 1968. In 1969, Steinberg's took a controlling interest in Phenix Flour, a firm it had invested in in 1967. (Mintzberg & Waters, 139)

The company took other diversification steps. Steinberg's went into the fast food business in 1962, opening a chain of drive-ins. This was followed by the purchase of a nearly insolvent chain of restaurants that operated in many Steinberg's shopping centers. In 1966, the Pik Nik chain of restaurants began under the leadership of Nathan's son, Lewis. The company opened a chain of gas stations in 1965, a chain of food stores in France in 1966, and pharmacies in 1969. None of these latter efforts was successful. According to *Topsy*, Sam Steinberg approved all these moves, but with decreasing knowledge. Several years after they purchased Cartier Sugar, Sam wanted to take a visitor to see it, and he had to ask where the business was located. (Mintzberg & Waters, 144-161)

At the same time that Miracle Mart was experiencing its problems, supermarket operations were also having difficulties. Competitive pressures had lowered prices and margins. Independent stores had grouped themselves into buying federations and were exerting even more pressure. The company's rate of growth in profits slowed in 1966, disappeared in 1967, and in 1968 profits fell by almost $1.5 million (Mintzberg & Waters, 150). See **Exhibit 3**.

7

Sam Steinberg

According to *Steinberg*, Sam was a unique retailing talent. His insatiable curiosity, his thirst for information about the business, and his deep-seated interest in serving the customer made Steinberg's a force to be reckoned with in the market. Executives would come from the U.S. to study what Sam was up to. Self-service meat and dairy departments, motorized conveyor belts at the checkout, and deliveries to the customers' cars were only a few of his innovations. (Gibbon & Hadekel, 81-84)

Arnold Steinberg described him as an excellent leader and engaging boss:

What Sam had going for him was enormous foresight and incredible charisma. No one could charm or give people the sense of belonging that he could. And it wasn't false—it was very genuine. He was great at rallying the troops. He was an incredible leader.

Jack Levine described Sam Steinberg as a chief executive who knew his company's and his own weaknesses and who worked diligently to overcome them in his quest to make Steinberg's "the best food retailer in Canada."

He knew his weaknesses. He hired Bob Cowan out of McGill University with an accounting degree. He worked for Sam for 50 years doing all the financial work.

At no time was he a store operator. He knew the business in the store, he understood it, but he didn't want to do the detail. He always visited the stores and became friends with the store managers. He wanted growth, and he knew that that meant real estate and building. He didn't want to be the biggest, but he wanted to be the best.

A long-time business associate of Sam's attributed his success to several factors:

At the time he began to grow, the community didn't know anything but steak, chops, and chicken. He introduced the U.S. way of retailing to Quebec. His competition was the corner grocery store. With his access to the states, he was able to use his contacts to really learn the way the industry was going.

He knew all the aspects of the retail business. He was beloved by his people. You have to be hands-on in this business, to motivate and challenge the employees, to notice what the customer is doing.

He did the thinking, and his team did the executing. He used his brothers for what they were worth, which wasn't much in most cases. He would make mistakes and pin them on others. The brothers understood perfectly that they were rich because of him. He was the one who organized his mother's store; he supported them all from the beginning.

Irving Ludmer believed that Sam was comfortable using his power and described one, not atypical, scene:

There would be meetings, and we would argue, and Sam would take a vote. If it was seven 'yes' and two 'no,' but Sam was with the no's, he would jokingly say 'the nays have it.'

8

He was open to others' ideas and was not threatened by people who disagreed with him. But you had to know the difference between disagreeing and threatening his authority. There was no room for that.

According to *Steinberg*:

> Sam acted more like a father than a brother. But what a father. Sam could intimidate them shamelessly, order them around, pick on them and blast them when they failed to carry out his instructions. He would dictate their every move. The brothers rarely fought back; they knew from an early age that he had it over them, just as they knew later on that he was largely responsible for their prosperity.... The intelligence, drive, marketing genius all went to one man. (Gibbon & Hadekel, 84-85)

One executive commented on the complicated set of relationships:

> The only reason it worked was that it was crystal clear that Sam was the boss. He had given pieces of stock to his brothers, at the beginning, and when the company went public, he demanded a voting trust agreement so that he would vote 100% of the stock. It was a formality, because they never would have challenged him. I asked one of his relatives once if they resented having given Sam all the control, and they replied, "Like I would have done so much better myself?" They were all always very grateful to him, and he was like the proud father, proud that his family had attained what it had through his efforts. And he never let them forget; they knew to whom they were indebted. He was pleased at what he had done for the family.

According to *Steinberg*, Sam ran the company with a paternalistic, controlling style: it was said that 250 people reported directly to him. There was a hard side to this approach. Sam could criticize and intimidate his employees to achieve the results he wanted. Sam Schuster, the company's longtime physician, remembered how proud Sam was of his toughness. "Once he fired a fellow, a big guy. Then he turned to me and said, 'Did you see me fire that guy?'" Schuster's theory was that Sam had a bit of a Napoleon complex. (Gibbon & Hadekel, 86, 88)

Still, Sam always had time to take a phone call from a store manager to discuss a problem or help out a loyal employee in financial straits. Indeed, it seemed that loyalty was a key quality at Steinberg's. One executive who had been particularly close to Sam left to go to J.C. Penney, the American retailer. Sam cut off communication with him for four years. "My departure was considered an extreme act of disloyalty.... It was like a son had married out of the faith." (Gibbon & Hadekel, 90)

Sam's style changed as the company grew. When the company was just in the grocery business in Quebec, Sam could maintain the kind of knowledge about the business of which he was justly proud. As it grew beyond this base, Sam's style changed along with the organization.

One long-time observer of the company commented on Sam's style:

> Sam let certain divisions have a great deal of freedom—like the sugar division. He knew he didn't know much about the sugar business. Therefore, he let whoever was running it do his job. He tried to manage everything, but discovered that his intelligence ran out when it came to manufacturing. He didn't know the sugar business so he left it alone.
>
> The trouble that Sam got into was that he wouldn't let all of his divisions have that freedom. He put his incompetent brothers in charge of other divisions, and

then maintained a high level of involvement. There was a funny attitude there: the family had the right to run a division even when it was clear that they weren't competent. They would stick a competent outsider in just below the family member. If the division did well, the family member took credit. If it did poorly, the other person took the blame.

One of Sam's subordinates described the changes in Sam's style that transpired over time:

> His style worked for a long time, but then Steinberg's simply became too big and too diverse. The company moved in directions where he had no skill and he knew it. He never understood the flour business, the sugar business, general retailing. Talking to 25 store managers on Monday morning wasn't going to do it in those businesses. He never had the patience to look at reports or figures. Paper was no good to him. In the early 1960s, there was a management committee of 15 to 25 people. They would meet Friday mornings and stay until everyone collapsed from hunger—2 or 3 in the afternoon. All the division and corporate managers were there. People would yell and scream like hell until they got an issue resolved. And all the decisions were made, and our batting average was very good.

> When he didn't know the business, he put good people there. He knew what he didn't know. I once heard him make the remark that he wouldn't hire himself as chairman of the company, now that it was so big.

The Organization

The simple functional organization that had evolved in the early 1930s remained in place for many years. By 1948, the number of stores had forced further articulation of store operations management. (See **Exhibit 4**)

As Steinberg's entered new businesses, new divisions were created, executives were appointed to run them. About 1960, the following appointments were announced: brother Nathan Steinberg was appointed executive VP, Max Steinberg was named VP and treasurer, Leo Goldfarb (Rita's husband) was named director of development and expansion, and Mel Dobrin (Mitzi's husband) was named VP of store operations. In 1962, Mel Dobrin, James Doyle (General Counsel), Leo Goldfarb, and Willie Sherman were named directors of the Corporation.

In 1964, Willie Sherman was appointed EVP in charge of Steinberg's corporate office, and he began to develop a formal structure at the head office. There was an attempt to separate the operations from the headquarters, as the head office was moved away from the headquarters of Quebec operations. One executive commented, "Before 1964, we didn't have structure, didn't have responsibility." (Mintzberg & Waters, 59-60)

As the company grew, there was an increased attempt to gain control of operations at the corporate level. Headquarters staff grew at a rapid rate. With the Ontario purchase there were now two divisions and separate corporate offices. Following the recommendations of a management consultant, power was centralized at headquarters. "Computers came in, manuals were written for store employees [16 in all], notions of "professional" management were pursued, and many of the staff groups in the food divisions were duplicated at headquarters." (Mintzberg & Waters, 137)

Yet, by 1967, the "huge bureaucracy" proved too uncomfortable for Sam Steinberg. "Willie attempted to contain Sam too much. Sam couldn't be in touch with the day-to-day business. In the

10

cases of conflict of interest—of which there were many—Sam was always on the side of the divisions. He was a store guy." (Mintzberg & Waters, 138)

One of Sam's executives described him this way:

> His heart was in the stores. He accepted and was able to live with "corporate management," but after he returned from a trip—or during a crisis—his first move was always to talk to the stores. His first morning back from a trip he would get on the phone and call 25 or so store managers to find out what was going on.

In the reorganization that followed, Mel Dobrin was appointed Executive VP of Retailing, and Willie Sherman took over the Miracle Mart Division. Jack Levine remained in charge of the Quebec Division.

The Family

Sam had an obvious interest in making his own family life very different from the experience he had as a youngster. As one close acquaintance described it:

> He had a miserable life growing up. His brother never wanted to work, and his mother's attitude was that you always whip the horse that got the job done. The store on the Main was never the same after Sam left it.

A member of the family described the early years as tough:

> In spite of what has been written about Ida, she was a terrible tyrant. No one could work with her. . . . Her husband was weak, and she and her sisters were strong. They had no use for him; the sisters drummed him out of the house.

Another long-time friend and observer remarked:

> His mother and father had split up. They had no father, and the family needed one, so Sam filled the role and acted it out. There was never a photo of the father anywhere—he was the black sheep who had let his family down. There **was** no father; Sam was it.

Sam and Helen's marriage was a very happy one. According to *Steinberg*, "Relatives say Helen, his first cousin, was the perfect wife for a man totally consumed by his business." (Gibbon & Hadekel, 93) Sam was devoted to her, and she to him. Moreover, he depended on her for everything from advice on dealing with the unions to laying out his clothes in the mornings. Helen played an unofficial, but important, part in the business. Executives recall her coming down in the middle of the night to union negotiations, or listening in on the telephone extension—at Sam's request—during his morning calls into the office. (Gibbon & Hadekel, 92-95)

Sam and Helen had begun a family in 1929, when a daughter, Mitzi, was born. Rita was born in 1932, Marilyn in 1933, and Evelyn in 1938. (Gibbon & Hadekel, end flap)

In 1942 Ida died, a victim of pneumonia. Vilmos had been living in Montreal since the unofficial divorce. Sam and his brothers had provided Vilmos with a modest stipend but saw him very rarely. He was never included in the frequent gatherings of the large extended family. With Ida's death, however, he came around a bit more and established a relationship with his grandchildren before he died in 1947. (Gibbon & Hadekel, 55-56)

Sam's other devotion was his business, and he combined his two passions in predictable ways. A Sunday drive with the family often meant a tour of potential Steinberg's locations. Friday night Sabbath dinners were a forum for family and business associates to talk about Steinberg's. One in-law recalled that business was always the topic at the Steinbergs. "At dinner time, at breakfast time, Sundays, and holidays. If you were part of the family and weren't part of the Steinberg organization, you almost felt like an outsider. . . . You felt like a deaf mute." (Gibbon & Hadekel, 97)

The girls were brought up in this traditional family environment. Sam provided for them in the way his parents never could for him. Gibbon and Hadekel report that "it is the impression of relatives and friends that the girls were spoiled rotten." Sam encouraged the girls to grow up to be like Helen—a dutiful wife and mother. He never encouraged them to go to University or to begin a career. (Gibbon & Hadekel, 95)

Steinberg reports that for all the happiness he got from his family, there was a disappointment. "When Helen gave birth to her fourth daughter, Evelyn, in 1938, Sam Steinberg did not pass out cigars. He lost his temper instead. When congratulatory colleagues asked him at the Hochelaga Street office whether his child was a boy or a girl, he responded by taking a kick at a twenty-foot stock cart. 'A girl,' he snapped, 'another girl.'" (Gibbon & Hadekel, 101)

Steinberg describes the family as:

> . . . . tremendously close. They went to Plage Laval beach together in the summers; they went to Palamino Lodge for the holidays. There was no occasion more wonderful than Helen and Sam's Friday night Sabbath suppers. When the daughters began to have their own families, they would gather . . . for Helen's delicious cooking, some lively conversation, and of course, Sam's stories about the business. (Gibbon & Hadekel, 95)

Indeed, in the mid 1950s, the Steinbergs appeared in *McCall's* magazine as the "Togetherness Family of the Month." (Gibbon & Hadekel, 174)

Mitzi described their relationship: "We never had a bad relationship. . . . But it wasn't the normal father-daughter close relationship. I was never home and neither was he. He'd be very tired and aggravated when he came home." (Gibbon & Hadekel, 156) The Steinberg daughters were growing up and getting married during this period, and their husbands entered the company.

Mitzi had married Mel Dobrin, an accountant, in 1949, and he had begun working for Steinberg's in 1950. Evelyn's husband, William Alexander, whom she had married in the early 1950s, was working in Steinberg's bakery business. Marilyn had married Len Pedvis in the mid-1950s. He worked for Steinberg's in a variety of capacities including butcher, store manager, and zone manager. Rita married Leo Goldfarb in 1950, and he proved to be a shrewd and effective business person. He was talented, bright, and was soon running Steinberg's real-estate arm. Leo was Mel Dobrin's best friend and, indeed, had met Rita through Mel. (Gibbon & Hadekel, 104)

There were tensions between the sisters, even at an early age. *Steinberg* reports that while Marilyn got along well with her father, she noticed an unusual relationship between her sister Mitzi and Sam.

> Every one of us had a super relationship with him except Mitzi. . . . She thought she was really challenging him. He knew it, he laughed, and he didn't fight her about it. Mitzi was always so different. Even when the kids went to summer camp, three of the sisters would go to one camp, and Mitzi would go to another. (Gibbon & Hadekel, 177)

Mitzi was also something of a tomboy, playing hockey and football with the boys, not the girls. By 1958, she had three children of her own.

As Sam Steinberg's daughters raised their families, their husbands progressed through the ranks of the business. By 1969 Mel Dobrin was Executive VP of Retailing, overseeing all foodstore and Miracle Mart operations. Marilyn's husband, Len Pedvis, had quit Steinberg's in the early 1960s after being passed over for a promotion. Marilyn and Len had divorced in the mid-1960s, and she had married a millionaire clothing merchant, Simon Cobrin. William Alexander was also working for Steinberg's. Leo Goldfarb had recently left after having run the real estate division. (Gibbon & Hadekel, 177)

There had been talk that Leo was the right man to succeed Sam, that he had Sam's winning personality and aggressive streak. Indeed, in *Steinberg*, it is reported that Sam decided that he wanted Leo to succeed him, but saw the problems with Mitzi and Mel looming. He asked Leo to do the "dirty work" of informing Mel, and Leo agreed. Mitzi and Mel took a firm stand against the move, and Leo backed off. He left the company several months later, in May of 1968. In 1969, he and Rita divorced. (Gibbon & Hadekel, 107-08)

The succession issue could not have helped the relationship between the sisters. *Steinberg* reports that there was always competition between the sisters and that it intensified as their husbands moved through the company. (Gibbon & Hadekel, 175) Mitzi was the unofficial leader, and observers commented on how she "lorded" over her siblings.

The Structure of Ownership

The company had gone public, but 52% of the voting shares were held by Sam and the trusts he controlled. In addition, he had a voting agreement with his brothers and in-laws that allowed him to vote 100% of the stock. Sam had worked with a well-known Canadian law firm to develop the ownership and inheritance structure of Steinberg's. Indeed, the approach was the same one that had been used by the Bronfmans for their ownership of Seagram. (Gibbon & Hadekel, 178)

Four identical trusts were established—one each in the names of his four children. The rationale for the trust approach was to avoid the payment of estate taxes upon the death of the stock's owner. By placing the stock in the trust early on, all of the increase in value accrues to the trust. Upon death, there is no change in ownership, so no tax is due. The four trusts each owned 25% of Rockview Investments, which in turn owned 2.4 million voting shares of Steinberg's (40% of the total). Another 12% of the voting stock was owned outright by Sam and was left to Helen in his will. Thus, the immediate family held 52%, and the rest of the family held the remainder of the voting stock. Rockview also owned slightly over 500,000 shares of the class A non-voting stock. (Gibbon & Hadekel, 178)

The trusts provided that the capital would be held for the benefit of the particular daughter until the eldest of her children reached the age of 25. At that point, 50% of the capital would be invested for the benefit of her children, in equal shares. These grandchildren could actually access the capital as follows: 50% of it at the age of 30, the other half at age 40. (Gibbon & Hadekel, 178-179)

There was a voting trust agreement that specified that all of the shares in the trusts and under Sam's ownership would be voted jointly. And as the daughters became adults (age 31), they all became trustees of their own—and of all the other—trusts. (Gibbon & Hadekel, 178-179)

Succession

The issue of succession was one that some members of the board had tried to get Sam to consider for some time. By 1969, the board included Sam himself, brother Nathan, nephew Arnold, sons-in-law Mel Dobin and Leo Goldfarb; Steinberg executives Jack Levine, James Doyle, and William Howieson; Sam's personal attorney Lazarus Phillips, industrialist Gerard Plourde, and financier André Charron.

The natural contenders for the presidency were all vice presidents of Steinberg's: Sam's brother, Nathan; Nathan's son, Arnold, a Harvard MBA; and Sam's son-in-law, Mel Dobrin. Jack Levine was also in the running. Yet, some felt that no one was up to the task. James Doyle, Steinberg's then general counsel, is quoted in *Steinberg* as saying, "None of the men near the top in the food end of the business were qualified to take over. . . . A lot of them were old-timers not capable of running a big corporation. Many non-family executives who might have been capable had left the company, believing that they had no future in such a family-dominated enterprise." (Gibbon & Hadekel, 103)

In March of 1969, Sam convened a three-day retreat of the company's senior managers to consider the issue of succession. Sam, at 64, had decided to step into the newly created post of chairman. (Gibbon & Hadekel, 108) He had to make a decision about whom to appoint as president.

Exhibit 1   Steinberg Family Genealogy

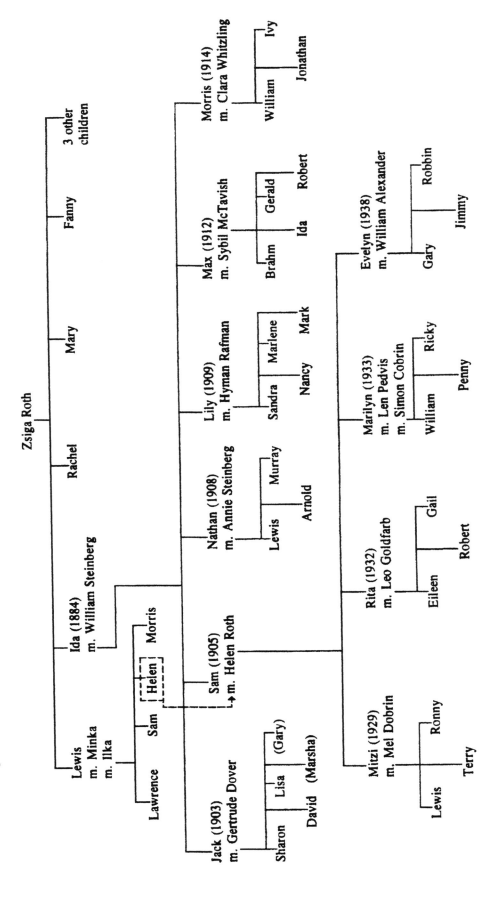

Source: Gibbon & Hadekel, front flap.   [Legend: m. = married; (date) = birth date; (name) = died as child.]

Exhibit 2   Comparison of Chain Store and Supermarket Economics in 1933 ($000)

	Typical Chain		Large Supermarket	
	$	%	$	%
Sales	54.00	100.0	2,000.00	100.0
Cost of goods sold	43.52	80.6	1,759.00	82.0
Gross margin	10.48	19.4	240.18	18.0
Expenses	9.67	17.9	166.00	8.3
Net profit	.81	1.5	74.18	9.7

Source: Tedlow, pages 234, 380

Exhibit 3   Steinberg Financials ($ Canadian)

Year	Number of Stores	Number of Employees[1]	Sales	Net Income	Approx. value of Common Equity (millions)
1931	6	NA	512,525	4,907	NA
1932	7	"	840,896	21,031	"
1933	8	"	1,471,629	(35)	"
1934	9	"	1,340,999	11,488	"
1935	11	"	1,865,972	13,075	"
1936	16	"	2,184,259	17,269	"
1937	19	"	3,365,491	26,480	"
1938	21	"	4,096,833	103,870	"
1939	23	"	4,758,729	212,323	"
1940	25	"	6,280,916	142,331	"
1941	28	"	7,945,303	93,587	"
1942	30	"	10,398,599	112,318	"
1943	30	"	10,489,882	122,564	"
1944	30	"	10,599,446	99,961	"
1945	30	"	12,837,887	163,261	"
1946	30	"	14,735,293	164,290	"
1947	31	"	18,747,954	386,166	"
1948	33	"	27,182,447	481,417	"
1949	34	"	36,197,230	591,417	"
1950	36	"	45,040,585	661,126	"
1951	38	"	58,182,060	845,685	"
1952	36	"	70,734,372	1,059,370	"
1953	38	"	80,373,003	1,450,932	"
1954	40	"	89,914,816	1,688,709	"
1955	49	"	101,753,994	1,783,697	"
1956	54	"	120,019,663	2,009,252	"
1957	59	5,000	132,431,428	2,397,023	"
1958	68	5,600	150,925,637	2,995,210	"
1959	115	6,300	178,261,413	3,392,785	72
1960	131	7,100	238,117,239	3,241,838	57
1961	140	8,000	253,222,229	3,817,692	82
1962	144	8,900	267,964,704	4,137,146	62
1963	147	10,000	286,809,909	4,801,471	62
1964	148	11,700	327,227,287	6,012,477	88
1965	154	14,900	379,096,946	7,134,626	146
1966	161	18,500	400,882,856	7,639,987	144
1967	166	17,000	439,495,953	7,698,308	130
1968	170	17,500	480,125,113	6,401,799	112

[1]Not available prior to 1957. Includes full- and part-time workers.

16

Exhibit 4　1948 Organization Chart

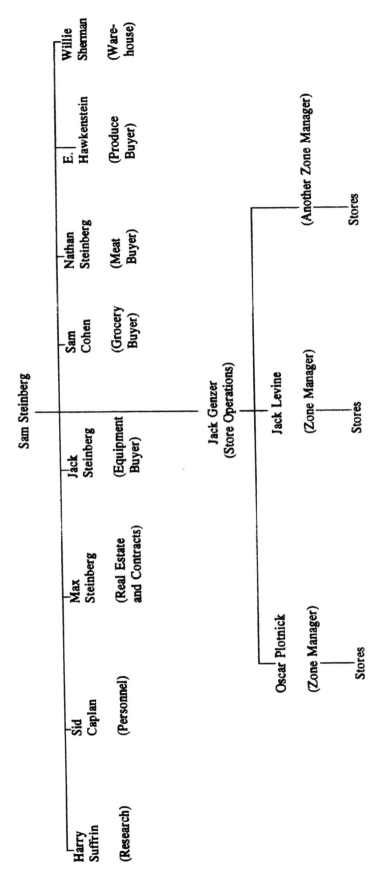

Source: Mintzberg & Waters, 57

Sam Steinberg (C)

(1969–1989)

On August 1, 1969, Sam announced his decision: Mel Dobrin would succeed him as president. One executive recalled hearing the news: "Sam made Mel president, but knew he wasn't up to the job."

Steinberg quotes one executive describing Sam's own explanation for the decision:

This is not the most qualified person we're selecting, Mel Dobrin. It may be in the best interests of the corporation to have a professional manager. But I've had so much fun building and running this business that I wouldn't deprive my family of running it." (110)

Leo Goldfarb, Sam's son-in-law, recalled a comment Sam had made when the two were travelling together on business:

That business was built specifically for my family. Anybody who wants to come in here, there's an open place for him. If the business is destroyed as a result of that, so be it." (110)

There was speculation that other factors had entered into the decision as well. "According to Jack Levine, Mitzi told him [Sam] that if Mel didn't get the presidency, she would move to Toronto." (110)

Mitzi was not surprised at the choice: "I don't even think he thought about who the best person was. Mel was the oldest daughter's husband. It was family." (110)

Professor Michael J. Roberts prepared this case with the assistance of Anthony G. Athos and Nan-b and Philippe de Gaspé Beaubien of the International Centre for Family Enterprises as the basis for class discussion rather than to illustrate either effective or ineffective handling of an administrative situation.

A note on sources: *Steinberg: The Break-Up of a Family Empire* by Ann Gibbon and Peter Hadekel (Ontario: MacMillan of Canada, 1990) proved invaluable in compiling this case on Sam Steinberg. Unless otherwise noted, page number references in this case refer to the Gibbon and Hadekel book. The reader should assume when a source is noted at the end of a paragraph that the material in that entire paragraph is based upon the source noted.

1

A board member spoke of the limited role the directors were able to play:

The outside directors gave him consistent advice about the problems with the steps he was taking, but he was the typical entrepreneur - he only heard what he wanted to hear. He was not a strictly rational man. He had succeeded with brute force and determination - with complete blinders with respect to a number of issues. He listened to the directors only so far as he wanted.

One executive looked back on the Palamino Conference and what transpired afterwards:

Palamino was really about Sam's agenda of getting the other executives to accept Mel, not about their getting him to listen to their ideas about succession. There was never any doubt. I remember being amazed that there were actually a couple of other guys making a run at it. Sam was trying to convince them about Mel, and he knew that it was not an easy sell. He felt that Mitzi and Mel together could run the company. Mel had been with him for a while by then, and Mitzi had the drive, so he thought it would be a good combination. The converse side is that by appointing Mitzi, through Mel, he could have it both ways. If she succeeded, she was a chip off the old block. If not, then the company had gone down with Sam. So he would win either way.

The board raised the succession issue, but went along with his desires. They went along with too much, in my view, and I remember asking one of the men on the board about it. He said, "You must remember that they had a control block - they had all the votes. Who am I to resign if this is what they want." There was never a perceived difference in incentive. The family wanted good returns on their voting stock just as much as the public wanted a return on its non-voting stock.

Another executive offered his perspective:

It [the Palamino Conference] ended up as a concerted effort towards the appointment of a professional manager as president. There had been several signs that Sam was moving in the direction of Mel. At the end Sam simply said, "It's my decision." It was clear to him how everyone felt, and also clear that Mel didn't have the capability. He believed that the organization had the ability to manage around him. And the organization would have survived had it not been followed up with Mitzi's involvement.

Mel was a nice guy. You could work with him and around him. He didn't interfere. Sam bypassed Mel regularly. Even with Mel's appointment things didn't change much for several years. Then, Sam began to be away more and for fairly long periods.

He would call everyday - it was a ritual. He would call at four, and whatever was going on would be discussed. There were three to six of us that would talk around the speakerphone. Jack Levine was clearly the leader in these discussions.

Jack Levine recalled his efforts to work with Sam on the succession issue:

> We tried to deal with it in '65, '66, '67; we met every Sunday for a while. I described all sorts of options. I gave them three or four models: a holding company to own all the shares but not voting at the board level, a board made up predominantly of outsiders that could have the power to outvote the family. I named names of who would be good on the board. But he wanted the family to have hands-on control of the company.

Shortly after Mel Dobrin's promotion, Jack Levine was appointed executive vice-president of retailing, and given the same job description as Mel. (112)

As a consequence of the succession decision, Steinberg's continued to lose talented executives to other firms where they felt they had a greater chance for advancement. Morgan McCammon, for instance, left and later became president of Molson Breweries. (112)

Shortly after the succession issue was resolved, Rita Goldfarb, Sam's second-oldest daughter, died of cancer at age 38. (117)

Mitzi Enters the Business

In 1973, Sam met Mitzi for lunch and complained about the performance at Miracle Mart, the discount department store chain. He offered her the job of turning the chain around. Mitzi was 43 and had never worked for Steinberg's before. But she plunged into the job. Sam had offered her the job over the objections of Jack Levine and other executives. Some suspected Mitzi had been pushing for a job at Steinberg's for some time. (158)

One executive recalled hearing the news:

> What made Mitzi dangerous was that she had many of her father's weaknesses but few of his qualities. Mel you could reason with, but not Mitzi. When she got her mind set on something, that was it. There was no talking with her. It was the beginning of the end.

Another senior manager was distraught:

> I couldn't understand it. He was a good judge of talent, but his daughters were different. He was a good husband but not a particularly good father. He just didn't make that much time.

Miracle Mart continued to lose money, although Mitzi got a lot of favorable press. She claimed that she was turning Miracle Mart around, but it was difficult to determine because its financial results were consolidated with the rest of Steinberg. She fired numerous managers, and those that remained lived in constant fear of her acerbic manner. (158-164)

3

One senior executive described the impact of Mitzi's appointment:

From this point onward, the bulk of top management's attention and energy was spent on conflict and containment. And once Mitzi was involved at Miracle Mart, she got involved in everything. She went through a lot of executives at Miracle Mart. We ended up spending a lot of time patching things up.

Before Mel was elevated, the family involved in the business was either competent or out of the way. But after this, there was a trilogy - Sam, Mel, and Mitzi.

But, the real estate and grocery business covered up a lot of mistakes for a lot of years.

Steinberg describes Jack Levine's reaction and subsequent discussions with Mitzi:

Jack, never one to couch his opinions in gentle terms, told Sam point-blank then that the decision was a rotten one. Later he told Mitzi herself that she didn't know how to handle people and that Miracle Mart was suffering as a result. He was taken back by her response. "She said, 'What are *you* talking about? I *was* captain of my golf club.'" (126)

The management team was disappointed that Sam had let family considerations en decision:

He never would have put one of his brothers in charge of Miracle Mart. He was aware of the problem with Mitzi, but he couldn't deal with it. A lot of families believe that the company is like royalty - the first-born inherits the crown, they inherit the business. He couldn't deal with it because it was so tied up with his own mortality.

Some say he had a death wish - I couldn't believe it then, but who knows, maybe it is true.

When we were young he used to say, "It doesn't matter what you do with the milk, you have to protect the cow." But once he got older, he didn't think that way.

The favorable publicity on Mitzi caught the eye of the Royal Bank of Canada, which was looking to add a woman to its board. Mitzi became a director, and her public profile rose. She was on government boards and was in demand as a speaker. She became a natural spokesperson for the company. (164-165)

Some thought that this was the role Mitzi had been working towards her whole life:

Mitzi was interested in proving to the world that *she* was the son Sam never had. She told stories about herself growing up that emphasized the "tomboy" side of her nature. She loved to play hockey and football, but only with the boys. She bragged about taking the punishment, and about dishing it out.

One executive gave his view of Mitzi's and Mel's involvement:

Did Sam *truly* understand the depth of their lack of ability - probably not. His attitude was that they're good enough and I'm around to be sure that everything is OK. As long as he was around, he would smooth things over. He was wrong about this though. There were serious problems that arose, and good people left. Mel was indecisive, and his main objective was not to make a bad decision that Mitzi would call him on the carpet for. .Mitzi was irrational and made decisions in rapid fire, but usually the wrong ones.

. She saw herself as his heir, as brilliant and able to see through situations and make the correct decision. She was the proverbial loose cannon. People were simply terrorized by her.

After Sam

On May 24, 1978, Sam Steinberg died at the age of 72. The family was shocked by his sudden death, and Steinberg's employees grieved openly for their boss. (119-120) Some thought that before Sam died, he realized the enterprise was headed for trouble: "He knew that leaving the stock split up the way it was would provoke a bloodbath."

Executives thought Sam too smart *not* to realize what was going to happen:

Sam could not but have known the actual impact of what he was doing. I was convinced that he had a death wish - "Apres moi le deluge" - although I am much less sure of this now.

Others thought his options limited:

Towards the end, he may have sensed that things were not going to go well, but what could he do - he didn't own the shares anymore.

When Sam died, the trustees of the family's holdings - each of the four trusts - were Mitzi and Mel Dobrin, Marilyn and Simon Cobrin, Evelyn and William Alexander, and Sam's youngest brother, Morris. (Rita had died in 1970.)

Barely two weeks after Sam's death, Mel Dobrin stepped up to the post of chairman, and Jack Levine assumed the presidency. As the new era began, the stores were on a downhill slide. New chains had made strong inroads in the Quebec grocery business, and its operations outside of groceries were faring poorly. (122)

Mitzi soon drifted away from her involvement in Miracle Mart, which was ultimately to cost Steinberg's $100 million. (160) She became more involved in the running of Steinberg's as a whole.

One executive commented:

While he [Sam] was still alive, the appointment of Mel really changed nothing. It was a holding pattern; nothing would change as long as Sam was around. But

5

once he was gone, Mel and Mitzi really took hold. This must have been his desire. If you get to be 70 and you haven't planned for the succession of the business, then this must be what you want. He knew he had a heart problem, and his brother had died in his 50s. So...it was a case of family loyalty blinding his judgement.

Jack Levine

Levine's acceptance of the presidency was based on one condition: that he have the full support of Mitzi Dobrin. Their past relationship had not been smooth, and she held a lot of the family power now that Sam was gone. It was tough to fill Sam Steinberg's shoes, and the situation with Mitzi didn't help matters. Some executives speculated that Mitzi was jealous of the relationship Jack had with her father. (126)

Steinberg relates that certain executives bypassed Levine, currying favor with Mitzi. Managers argued over decisions, invoking Sam's name and maintaining that he would want things done a certain way. Meetings turned into shouting matches, the decision-making process was disorganized, and store renovations ceased. As the industry became more competitive, the company's performance deteriorated. (126-128)

In 1982, Jack Levine announced his retirement, and Steinberg's was again looking for a leader.

Peter McGoldrick

The choice of the company's next president was made by Mitzi and Mel. They selected Peter McGoldrick, then chairman of a small chain of foodstores in Virginia.

One executive commented on the choice:

It was Mitzi's dream that she would run the company through Mel. The family would not agree to Mitzi as president, so McGoldrick made a good choice. He was the puppet, and Mitzi could pull the strings. The board would never have agreed to her as president.

But 17 months into his 5-year contract, McGoldrick resigned. A new marketing program had become a fiasco, costing the company millions. And McGoldrick had not had an easy time with Mitzi either. Shortly after he took over, Mitzi informed him that she would be moving into the head office as executive vice-president for corporate and legal affairs. (167)

Irving Ludmer

The company was again looking for a president, and this time, turned to Irving Ludmer. Ludmer had run the Ivanhoe real estate subsidiary, but had quit in 1971. Ludmer was named president in April of 1984 and, in the space of 18 months, had engineered a turnaround. (146-147)

6

Still, *Steinberg* reports, Ludmer and Mitzi had problems:

> It seemed that every time Ludmer made a decision, Mitzi would go home and tell her husband Mel, the Steinberg's chairman, about it. The next day the decision would be undone. Company executives did not know where to turn for direction. (153)

Ludmer had the full backing of Steinberg's outside directors, and he was not willing to operate in such a mode. *Steinberg* reports that it was not long before Ludmer became frustrated and ". . . made it clear he would quit if his authority continued to be undercut." Mitzi resigned in September of 1985. (170)

Ludmer's position was bolstered by the firm's performance: After 18 months, Steinberg's stock had gone from $12.50 to $50, and profits had climbed 5-fold from 1984 to 1985. (147)

Family Disagreements

According to one long-time advisor, once Mitzi had left Steinberg's, she wanted to sell the business:

> After she had left the company, Mitzi didn't want anyone to succeed with it. And why put all your money into a business in Quebec when French nationalism was so strong?

Steinberg quotes Simon Cobrin, Marilyn's husband, as saying, "One day Mitzi left Steinberg's. The next day she moved into the family office and started taking over." (183)

The first sign that the daughters' interests might be diverging came when Mitzi informed her sister Marilyn in late 1985, shortly after she had resigned, that she had arranged a meeting in New York with someone who might be interested in buying Steinberg's. The discussion proved fruitless, but Mitzi continued to seek out potential buyers. (181-182)

Mitzi argued that she was uncomfortable having so much of the family wealth tied up in a single asset - Steinberg's shares - that were paying a dividend that represented a return of 1 percent on investment. (217) Mitzi began to advocate the position that the trusts should dispose of their publicly traded non-voting stock, but the other sisters were not interested. So, Mitzi began to argue that the sisters should resign from each others' trusts and simply manage their own money. (182-183)

Some saw the arguments as an expression of long-harbored ill-will between the sisters:

> The sisters had a lot of bottled-up rage towards Mitzi. Once she was out of the company, she just wanted the money to do other things to prove that she was a chip off the block.

As Mitzi became more involved in the family office, Marilyn became upset, feeling as though she was being pushed out of her longtime role as trust administrator and head of the family investments. As the battle wore on, the sisters began to accuse each other of conflict of interest.

Evelyn joined forces with Marilyn. *Steinberg* reports that she had blamed Mitzi for the fact her husband - William Alexander - had never gotten ahead at Steinberg's. (176) Marilyn and Evelyn refused to allow Mitzi to sell any of the non-voting stock in her trusts, yet in the Spring of 1986, they were selling Class A stock that they owned personally. Mitzi charged that their decision was motivated by their desire not to depress the price of the stock they were selling themselves. (185)

The Dobrin children - two of whom were lawyers - began to press Marilyn to distribute the income and dividends from their share of the trusts. In 1987, they made a formal request that the trusts distribute their share of the capital. Marilyn resisted and told the family that she would no longer have anything to do with the Dobrins. (186)

By this time, there were often 25-30 family members at family meetings, and it was clear that there was a wide disparity of views among the group. Some wanted the company preserved as a family enterprise, while others wanted to cash out. (217)

The dispute wore on, and Evelyn and Marilyn tried to remove the trust's long-standing legal advisors and replace them with another law firm. Helen, who had long tried to remain above the dispute, finally put her foot down, saying the firm had been loyal and had served the family well. Marilyn stopped speaking to her mother, and she and her husband refused to attend Helen's 80th birthday party. (186-187)

Marilyn and Evelyn asked Ludmer for seats on the board. It seemed wrong to them that the Dobrins should have two seats while they had none. Mitzi and Mel, who had long represented the family's interests on the board, were insulted. The sisters were rebuffed, however, and so in December of 1986 they began buying shares from other relatives in an attempt to increase their control. Mitzi viewed this as a clear breach of their duty as trustees. (188)

In an attempt to assuage the sisters, Mitzi and Mel had allowed Marilyn's and Evelyn's husbands to become directors of Rockview, the holding company for the family's 12% stake that was not in the daughters' trusts. (184)

Now that they were directors, Marilyn and Evelyn began outvoting Mitzi and Mel, and in 1987 authorized Rockview to separate its 40% holding in Steinberg's voting shares from Helen's 12%. Thus, the family holdings would no longer be voted together. The news was made public, and the stock market was concerned about who was really at the helm of Steinberg's. (189-190)

To those who knew the sisters, it was not surprising that there was a rift:

> Sam's daughters never adopted his family culture because that was not *their* culture. Sam grew up in the eastern European Jewish ghetto mentality where you had to stick together. That was simply not the girls' experience.

> People knew the level of sibling rivalry that existed between them. There was a great deal of rivalry between Mitzi and Marilyn. Mitzi thought that as the eldest, she was the designated heir. Marilyn resented being lorded over by Mitzi, and thought she was just as capable. When Marilyn challenged Mitzi, Mitzi could simply not comprehend it. She was their leader.

8

The trust structure was a disaster. It would have been much wiser to just give the kids their own stock and let them blow it if they wanted to. However, from a financial point of view, it did achieve a significant control premium.

The arguments became public at the same time that Steinberg's financial performance was declining - 1986 profits of $39 million were roughly half those of the previous year. The stock fell and the company became an attractive acquisition target. (188-191)

Ludmer was attempting to reconcile the factions because he recognized the impact their fighting was having on the public perception of the company. At the same time, however, he was also reorganizing the company, with occasional waves of lay-offs. Ludmer had always fought the nepotism he observed at Steinbergs, and he fired several family members, including Lewis (Nathan's son) and David (Jack's son). In 1988 he fired Marilyn's son, Billy, and the whole family was upset, feeling that Ludmer had betrayed them. (199)

Some family members had seen Billy as the natural heir. He had graduated with an economics degree and had spent more than 10 years at Steinberg's. Billy was very public in his ambition to become the next president of Steinberg's. (198-199)

Ludmer commented on the incident:

> When I concurred with the firing of Marilyn's son, it turned her against me. I felt I had no choice. My men came to me and said that he had to go. If I had not concurred, I would have been sending the signal that the company really had not changed.

Still the fighting got worse, with Marilyn and Evelyn exercising their control over Mitzi and Helen's shares at every possible turn. Finally, just after Christmas in 1987, Mitzi filed suit against Marilyn and Evelyn, claiming "gross negligence and reprehensible disregard" in their management of the trusts. The suit contained several personal attacks on the Cobrins and Alexanders, alleging that Marilyn had no education, that the husbands were "little more than putty in their wives' hands," and that there was considerable conflict between Helen's wishes and those of Marilyn and Evelyn. (204-205)

One family member saw the lawsuit as an expression of Mitzi's rage with her sisters:

> She sued her sisters out of rage that they would question her judgement. She never understood how she had lorded over them.

The suit contained enough details of the family's squabbling to make it in front page news. Now, Steinberg's directors were alarmed. The family squabble was making it increasingly difficult to get on with business. The board invited bids for the company as a way to end the dispute. One board member was quoted as saying, "You can't run a company like this while the controlling shareholders are at each others' throats." (208)

As the possibility of a sale became evident, the stock market turned to a new concern. Because of the structure of voting and non-voting shares, it was possible for someone to buy complete control of Steinberg's by purchasing the family's voting shares, leaving the public shareholders out in the cold, in spite of the fact that the public non-voting shares comprised 71 percent of the total equity. (208, 217)

Between 1982 and 1988, the composition of Steinberg's board had become decidedly less insider dominated. Arnold Steinberg and Mel and Mitzi Dobrin remained as inside directors. Donald Campbell, a prominent businessman, André Charron, head of a major investment firm, and J. Raymond Cyr, president of Bell Canada, remained as outside directors. Arnold's father, Nathan, had died and Jack Levine and James Doyle had retired. They were replaced by Irving Ludmer and four outside board members. Thus, the board had swung from six insiders and five outsiders to four insiders and seven outsiders.

Takeover

Shortly after the board decided to accept bids, one emerged. On January 25, 1988, a trio of investors - in a partnership called Oxdon - announced that they were making a $980 million bid for Steinberg's. It was clear that these were classic "raiders" who would borrow the money to make the bid and then dismantle the company in an attempt to pay back their debt. (211)

Ludmer was upset, and began his own efforts to put together a bid for a management buyout. Arnold Steinberg was interested, and the two joined forces. Ludmer looked at selling the Quebec grocery business - which Oxdon would have sold anyway - as a way to raise money to buy in the family shares. The unions were alarmed at the prospect and pleaded with Steinberg not to sell. They agreed to lower their wages to make the division more profitable, and the company announced that it was no longer for sale. Oxdon had acquired an 8% or so stake in the company, and it bided its time on the sidelines. (216-218)

In the meantime, the sisters pursued the possibility of a leveraged buyout. A meeting was scheduled with Ludmer to discuss the possibility, but Ludmer opposed them, claiming the turnaround was proceeding well. Now Ludmer's decision to fire Marilyn's son came back to haunt him. The meeting reinforced the notion that Mitzi had been trying to convince her sisters of all along - Steinberg's wasn't a family company anymore, it was just an investment controlled by someone else. Evelyn and Marilyn finally saw things Mitzi's way, and following the meeting with Ludmer, met among themselves and agreed to sell the company. (229-231)

In March of 1989, Oxdon reared its head again, making a new offer for the company. Oxdon announced its plans for the company, which included selling the grocery stores to Loblaw's, the Ontario concern. While the sisters wanted to sell, the Oxdon proposal was unappealing because they were offering the same price for the Class A non-voting as for the sisters' voting shares. The sisters felt they were entitled to a premium. (232-234)

In the meantime, Ludmer began looking for a buyer of his own. If the company was to be sold, better it be sold to someone who was not so openly hostile. Ludmer found the Caisse de depot et Placement du Quebec, the $35 billion government pension fund. The two parties began to talk about a deal. (235)

At the same time, another Montreal financier - Michel Gaucher - began talking to the sisters about buying their shares at the $75 figure they had said was their asking price. Gaucher lined up a $1.5 billion bridge loan from Merrill Lynch on the strength of the Ivanhoe real estate. (235-239)

Ludmer's talks with the Caisse were going poorly because they wanted him to sell Ivanhoe's real estate - to them. So, the Caisse began to negotiate with Gaucher about buying the real estate from him if he ultimately bought Steinberg's. They came to an agreement under which the Caisse would finance Gaucher's acquisition. (242-246)

Gaucher made his offer official: $75 for the voting shares and $50 for the Class A shares. On top of the offer, the Gaucher/Caisse proposal played on the sisters' emotion about keeping the company under Quebec ownership. Finally, the sisters agreed, negotiating a $1 increase in the price the public would be paid for its shares. (248-253)

But the fight wasn't over. Oxdon announced that it would pay $53 for the Class A shares. Now the board was in a quandary. The outside directors, in particular, had a problem. Their duty was to represent all of the shareholders, not just the family. They had no choice but to recommend Oxdon's bid. This, in turn, created a problem for Gaucher, who needed two-thirds of *each* class of stock to take the company private. (258)

When Gaucher finally released the details of his bid, it didn't help his case. He and his partners were putting in a very small amount of their own money - $20 million or so. Oxdon sued the Gaucher/Caisse group, arguing that the financing arrangements of the deal really meant that the Caisse was acquiring the company, something it was forbidden to do by its charter. (258-261)

After the suits and countersuits wound their way through the courts, and after the shareholders had tendered their shares, Gaucher had 100% of the voting stock, but less than 30% of the Class A shares. Finally, during the summer of 1989 the Oxdon group agreed to sell its stake to the Gaucher/Caisse group, realizing that it could not compete against this quasi-governmental entity. The deal was consummated in August of 1989. Each of the sisters' trusts owned approximately 1.5 million shares, which were cashed out for over $112 million apiece. (262-265)

Aftermath

One observer close to the family saw the sisters' actions in a poor light:

> When the takeover came and the girls fought for more money than the non-voting shareholders, it was terrible. Sam would never have taken more for himself. He was not attached to material things. He was driven by pride in his accomplishments and the respect of the community. The minority shareholders were always treated just like the others in all of the deals he was in. It was the same in the real estate projects.

> He left his trusts to the girls and they got greedy, grasping the money for themselves. They didn't want advice - they just listened for the sweetest siren's song.

> He never gave them an education, and, with one exception, they married weak husbands. The trusts were put in place for tax reasons. The Bronfmans had them so he wanted them. They have wreaked nothing but havoc in most cases.

He never viewed it as a public company - it was a family business. After he was gone, there was a feeling that it was OK as a family business as long as it was being well-managed by the family. Once that started to break down, it was all over.

Irving Ludmer offered his perspective:

There were poor Steinbergs before Sam and there will be poor Steinbergs again (and the same is true for my family). Part of the game is to give the children what they want and give them the freedom to blow it. Sam and the whole family would have been better off if he had let go. He clearly had the option to do a lot of things - placing all the voting stock in one person's hands, strengthening the board, rewriting the trust - but he chose not to.

* * *

Soon after the takeover, Steinberg's fringe operations were sold off, but the Quebec supermarket operation remained a going concern. By 1992, however, the debt that had been taken on to finance the acquisition proved crippling. The company went bankrupt, costing the Caisse (the government pension fund) nearly $800 million, according to some estimates. Seventy-five years after Ida had first opened her store on "The Main," Steinberg's no longer existed.

Exhibit 1   Steinberg Financials ($ Canadian)

Year	Number Stores(a)	Number Employees	Sales (millions)	Net Income (millions)	Approx.value of Common Equity (b) (millions)
1969	178	18,000	553	5.9	82
1970	180	20,000	679	9.3	95
1971	182	22,000	786	9.5	123
1972	185	23,000	872	15.0	182
1973	187	23,000	1,012	16.7	162
1974	191	23,000	1,197	16.3	128
1975	196	23,000	1,430	12.3	125
1976	197	24,000	1,605	21.4	115
1977	206	24,000	1,767	21.7	134
1978	209	24,000	1,922	27.1	112
1979	218	25,000	2,033	26.8	169
1980	224	26,000	2,192	27.9	167
1981	247	31,000	2,751	39.5	220
1982	246	31,000	3,210	34.1	195
1983	242	32,000	3,248	13.4	210
1984	241	32,000	3,341	15.0	188
1985	239	32,000	3,801	73.6	225
1986	227	35,000	4,042	38.9	687
1987	217	31,000	4,491	66.9	684
1988	200	26,000	4,585	(17.9)	761

(a) Canadian and U.S. Grocery Stores.
(b) Includes voting and non-voting common stock.
Source: Mintzberg & Waters, Page 67, and Steinberg's Annual Reports, and Moody's.

Sam and Helen

Source: Mr. Sam, private edition

Sam receiving the order of Canada

Source: Mr. Sam, private edition

Bibliography

Gibbon, Ann and Peter Hadekel. *Steinberg: The Break-Up of a Family Empire.* Ontario: MacMillan of Canada, 1990.

Carmen Bianchi Family Business Associates
14758 Caminito Punta Arenas
Del Mar, CA 92014
Phone: 858-922-3155 or 858-793-2445
Email:cbianchi@familybizconsulting.com
www.familybizconsulting.com

The Keys to Succession: Questions that <u>Should</u> be Answered.

1. Who are the MOTIVATED SUCCESSORS? Do they possess knowledge and experience beyond that of the founder?

2. Is there AN ORGANIZED AND HARMONIOUS TEAM OF MANAGERS? Do they approach the responsibility professionally? Do they agree to accept the new leadership enthusiastically?

3. Are there COMPETENT ADVISORS who understand the business, know and respect the successors? Are they willing and capable of helping pilot the business through the unchartered waters ahead?

4. Is there AN UNCOMPLICATED AND RATIONAL OWNERSHIP STRUCTURE, one which does not confuse inheritance with management?

5. Are the HEIRS ACCOMMODATING to the neds of each other? Can they cooperate and work together or agree to separate themselves from the enterprise? (Business is tough enough without having to pull your punches in order not to upset sectors of the ownership!)

6. Is there a truly WORKING BOARD OF OUTSIDE DIRECTORS? (The presence and influence of which is an even greater requirement than there ever was for the founder.)

7. Does the outgoing owner/manager have a plan for MEANINGFUL CONTRIBUTION AFTER RETIREMENT that does not interfere with the long-term strategy of the company?

8. Does the ESTATE PLANNING of the controlling stockholders effectively recognize the future realities of both family and business needs?

These are the keys to a smooth succession. When they exist in a business founder's departure, successors only have to face the huge complexities and problems of ensuring that a successful, growing company continues to succeed and grow in an increasingly complex world.
If these keys are not present and, sadly, they too often are not – the successors also face the monumental task of putting them in place – if it is not too late.

Leon Danco Ph.D.

Succession

A Succession plan is as important as having :
An Estate Plan
A Financial Plan
A Strategic Plan

Good succession/transition should encompass all four plans. Every closely-held and family business company should have an exit strategy-What is yours?
Is your exit strategy written down or is it in your head? Are you willing to sell your company and if not why not?
Could it be that your company is your legacy and that your dream is to perpetuate it through the generations? But whose dream is it anyway because if it is not your next generations dream then your company may become a part of the statistics that say 92% of all companies in the USA are family owned and/or closely held but by the 2nd generation this drops to 34% and by the 3rd generation to 16%. BEWARE!! ! Shirt sleeves to shirt sleeves in 3 generations could become your legacy! If your successor does not have that fire in the belly, he/she is not going to succeed and he/she is certainly not going to successfully steward the company through to the next generation.

 Once you have established who the successors are going to be then the next stage would be *Leadership Development*. Successors acquire the needed leadership skills and experience and are acknowledged by employees and clients as the ones who will succeed. The final stage would be the *Transition*. This should be accomplished naturally to avoid ripples that could derail the succession.

Additional issues facing the success of any plan would be:

- What will the ownership roles (if any) of family members who are not active in the business?
- If succession is split between two or more siblings and/or family members, what agreements should exist between shareholders that will allow for future changes e.g. Buy/Sell agreements?
- Will minority ownership be allowed outside the family such as key employees, in-laws, public offerings?
- Planning for transition to the next generation
- Values and skills which the next generation will need in order to be prepared to accept the responsibility of caring for the family business.
- What steps would be needed to help the next generation acquire these skills?

Suggestions for Successor Development

- Assure yourself that family business entry is voluntary
- Get meaningful, full-time outside work experience
- Enter with a specific, needed, precedented job description and pay level
- Prepare for a job that doesn't exist yet
- Be prepared to work harder than others in the company
- Update your written personal development plan yearly
- Review personal development plan with parents, siblings and key business advisors
- Look for mentors inside and outside the business
- Seek the presidency of an organization outside of work
- Develop a peer group of young business presidents and family successors
- Identify leadership models to emulate
- Take jobs in a variety of functional areas
- Volunteer to make presentations to the Board
- Hire, evaluate and fire people as appropriate
- Consider formal testing of current aptitudes, strengths and needs
- Invest time in shared non-business interests with family
- Attempt to write down the company's key strategic policies, management philosophies and cultural values
- Remember that real authority comes from earning respect, not from power
- Eventually identify your own future management team
- Be a role model of listening skills, openness and change

Finally, what we encourage is "The Ethical Will." We use this tool to communicate the most sensitive issues of succession- issues that deal with retirement, death, legacies, family values and love. These issues are passed on through the generations by an "Ethical Will."

Running a Business Like a Business

Highly functioning families that are in business together generally display some traits in common. For instance, they run the *family* as a family, run the *business* as a business and skillfully communicate; and maintain a reservoir of trust. These traits strengthen the relationships in the family and the business.

A *business-first* business operates in a professional manner and the family is an asset to the company.

"Business first" families support what is best for the company, its customers, employees and shareholders. They select sound business principles to govern hiring, compensation, and titles. They reason that such principles are fair and constitute excellent criteria by which to make tough decisions that will affect the entire family. They are willing to abide by these principles even if they lead to unequal treatment of family members or to selling the business.

WHERE DOES CONTINUUM FIT?

	FAMILY FIRST	BUSINESS FIRST
EMPLOYMENT	There is a job for all family members	If you're qualified to do the job, you can join
COMPENSATION	Family members are paid more than market rate for the job	Pay is determined by responsibilities and performance
LEADERSHIP	Leadership is bestowed. Title/office bestowed by birthright	Leadership is earned. Company officers control day-to-day operations
RESOURCES	Business resources are used for family perks	Strategic resources are used for business purposes
TRAINING/EXPERIENCE	Outside experience may be less valuable than years of service in the family business	Outside experience is more important than years of service in the family business

24

The Need for the Family Council

A Family Council is the organizational and strategic planning arm of a family, where all members meet to decide values, policy, and direction for the future. At the core, the Council is the vehicle to address and explore family concerns that influence the business and the family. It also defines, clarifies, and expresses the family's deepest values, meaning, mission, and legacy. By forming a Council, a family realizes that it is a large, important institution, whose decisions and activities influence not only its immediate members, but also employees and the community.

As we've explored in previous chapters, family businesses create too many complex issues for the family to leave them to random gatherings or the will of a single person. Many disputes that seem like pure business issues can only be resolved by the family. Investing in a new plant, promoting a non-family manager to CEO, selling or splitting the business, all relate to family interests. That is because, while the situation occurs within the business, it concerns issues that have to do with the family's connection to the business. Without a Family Council this process goes on informally and secretly in most family businesses. The Family Council makes these decisions open and explicit.

As we've seen, many families mistakenly feel that the best way to promote harmony is to avoid discussion of upsetting topics: if Billy is feeling upset because he thinks Dad favors Joey, the best way to deal with the situation is to ignore it. But in reality, if it is not discussed, Billy and Joey only get more estranged, while Dad remains ignorant of the unintended rivalry. A Family Council is the most effective forum to discuss such hurts. Very few issues get resolved by ignoring them.

The Council is also an acknowledgement that old-fashioned patriarchy is dead. Father can no longer unilaterally decide everything of importance for the family. The first son doesn't always inherit the business, and values, concerns, and conflicts among family members can't always be anticipated and mediated by the caring autocracy of the founder-patriarch. A Council recognizes that more participation, openness, information sharing, debate, and democracy are needed in today's complex family environment. Like Stan, the founder has to find out what people want. Without active commitment and involvement of all family members, he may risk deeply hurt feelings or mis-communication. Even though Dad may remain "head" of the family, and make the final decisions in some areas, increasingly families need to get everyone together to share information, feelings, and goals.

The business is the engine that serves the deeper needs of the whole family. The business often expresses the personal entrepreneurial dream of the founder or founding couple. A founder creates a business not simply to make money, but as a form of social expression about something he or she believes in. The business grows not just in size, but to a fuller or lesser expression of an idea. That is why a family squabble about the future of a company like Esprit, between the married couple who founded it, is so difficult to resolve. The debate among the two owners was not just about power or profits, but about the soul, the meaning of the company. When that dream passes to others—professional managers, heirs, or public stockholders—will it continue to hold the original founder's vision?

A founder's vision is only one of the stories contained in the family business. The business is also about the family's development, struggles, and successes. It is where the children help out after school, and what the family is known for. It is where sons and daughters dream of working, something that everyone in the family is often excited about. The business can be so much a part of the meaning of the family that all family members need to explore how the business is working for them. As part of the family, even though not part of the management of the business, they have strong opinions and exert influence. Usually they do it indirectly, to spouses in the business, or through others. In a Family Council, this influence comes out in the open.

Every family is judged personally by what its business does in the community. It isn't only having wealth, but what the family does with its wealth, that creates the measure of the family. The business often provides goods or services to the community, and hires people to work there. If the company is unfair to employees, sells shoddy merchandise, pollutes, or does not serve the community, the non-participating family members will hear about it. Children may be confronted in school. The whole family is a part of what the business means to the community.

Every family member has a different experience of the meaning and purpose of the family business. While parents want their children to echo their social and political views, in practice this almost never occurs. Those in the business see it one way, while those waiting in the wings deciding whether to enter the business, or those outside it, see it differently. These differences are not academic. There are points in every family and business where the stakeholders have to make a clear choice—about direction, about inheritance, about succession, or any number of other issues. When the choice has to be made who makes it, and how is it made? How is the input solicited from all those involved, who may not be formal decisionmakers but are deeply affected by the outcome? Some form of organized family gathering is necessary at these pivotal points in time to communicate, to explore differences, to arrive at decisions, and to implement them.

A Family Council also provides the forum for discussion of how the family uses its wealth and provides for all its members. The returns on a business can be generous, even enormous. It can create substantial wealth. It also leads to difficult questions:

- How will that wealth be passed on to the children?
- How can the parents live after retirement?
- What portion of the wealth should be returned to the community, and how should the remainder be invested?
- What values does the family want to express through the power and influence of its investments?
- How should family members who are part of and not part of the business be compensated?
- Should its wealth remain in the business, or should the family's business investment diversify and become more liquid?

As owners of the business, the family has the capacity to put their wealth and influence into the service of a wide variety of social goals. Family business theorist Will McWhinney notes that some families see themselves as stewards of the business, rather than owners.[1] Whereas ownership means simply having control of wealth, stewardship implies that the ownership exists for a broader purpose.

Many families express a social vision through business. Max DePree, son of the founder of Herman Miller, and the late Bill Gore, with his wife Genevieve, saw their respective companies as embodying their beliefs in participatory management. Everyone in each company is an owner, shares in the profits, and, in Herman Miller, is covered by a unique Employee Bill of Rights. McWhinney points out that the opportunity for such stewardship is limited in publicly-traded stock companies, because they are required to maximize stockholders' profit, but are unlimited in closely-held family businesses. (Indeed such economic limitations cause family businesses like Levi Strauss to take their company private.) The Family Council is the place where children learn about their stewardship, and where heirs and relatives can explore the nature of their family values and commitments.

The Nature of the Family Council

A Family Council is a planning tool for growing the family, its individual members, and the business controlled by the family. The Council is not a single meeting, but rather a regular forum for consideration of the complex issues facing a family in business. It's an ongoing process that formalizes informal exchange among family members. Family members share what they believe and what they want from the family and the business.

The key functions of the Council are communication and clarification of policies. Specifically the Family Council is the focal point for developing, sharing and implementing three types of future planning, corresponding to the three complex human systems that are part of it:

Individual Plans: As we've seen, each person in the family is growing, maturing, and continually redefining personal, career, and family goals. Each family member is at a different stage of his or her individual life cycle and needs distinct things from the family and the business. These individual needs can act at cross-purposes. The Council can help individuals discover what they want, by exploring possibilities and options, and help balance the needs of each individual with the family's and business' needs.

Family Plans: The family has its own developmental cycle: it is formed, raises children, matures, plans for retirement. Members are more closely connected at certain stages, more separated and far-flung at others. What are the overall goals of the family for the future, and what resources does it need to achieve them? How are the different branches of the family related, and how do new people enter the family? The family needs to plan to provide for each of its members, look at its basic values, and create a set of family rules about its wealth and participation in the business and other family enterprises.

Business Plans: The ownership of all or most of the business lies within the family. As people retire, and heirs decide whether or not to enter the business, ownership and management control may move from the family to outside managers and owners. The family's business can diversify from one enterprise to many, or one or more family members can take over control or ownership. In order for the business to be free to chart its course, family involvement needs to be clarified, changes need to be explored, and they need to be communicated and implemented in a timely manner.

The Family Council is the perfect vehicle for generating, sorting through, ratifying, and implementing each of these plans. Naturally as new challenges are presented, and as people grow and develop, new questions arise for consideration. Because the three planning entities are all interconnected, each plan affects the others. One son cannot plan his personal future without being part of the family and business plan. He needs to know whether he can expect to inherit a share of the business, whether he can count on the family to support him to start his own business, and when he needs to make a decision.

A Council can take many forms. It can be a formally constituted organization, with minutes, regular meetings, and prescribed decisions. Or it can be a more casual grouping, meeting intensely during a period of transition and informally at other times. Resource people and advisors can be brought in to help. The Council usually meets regularly, most often once a month for an afternoon or evening. It may include a weekend retreat once or twice a year. The retreat format is common when a family is scattered around the country and needs to fly in for meetings. These can be around holidays, but the Council meeting should be separate, an organized affair with records, a charter, and formal procedures.

The Council is a decision-making group. While power is handled differently in different families, most Councils work on a consensus model. Each person has a different role and involvement in the business so a simple majority is often not practical. When the issues concern ownership of the business, they often lie in the hands of one person or a small group. In that case the Council usually advises or suggests policy, but the owners make the final decisions.

The business founder, or head of the family, often has reservations about whether his legitimate authority over business decisions will be undermined, or challenged, by the Council. This is a difficult issue, that takes time to clarify and explore. Creating a Council is a recognition that there needs to be more collaboration in a family than has existed in the past. The Council can be an advisory group. The purpose is to make decisions explicit, to communicate more clearly, and to make processes that are done informally, behind the scenes, clearer to everyone. That should in fact reinforce the authority of the family leader.

I point out to concerned patriarchs that the Council does not take away authority, but rather recognizes that it is already limited. For example, in many family businesses, the wife of the owner, and mother of the heirs, is a power behind the throne. (As one NFL football coach, asked about why he employed his son as an assistant coach, replied to the media, "I didn't hire him because he is my son. I did it because I'm married to his mother.") The Council makes her role more explicit.

Convening a Family Council: Overcoming Resistance

How do you get a Council started? If the founder/owner is committed to the process, everything can proceed smoothly. The family business leader realizes that the time has come to share information and control. He calls a meeting of everyone in the family to start the ball rolling. But it's rarely so simple!

Since it seems so reasonable to have family input and participation in business as well as family issues, why do so few families naturally create a family forum to discuss these things regularly? The most frequently cited reason is the tendency of the family patriarch/business leader to keep such things to himself. Over the years, the entrepreneurial prerogatives of the family leader can harden into a set of attitudes that effectively seals off the patriarch not only from other family members, but from potential crises, personal pain, business shifts, and the need to change.

Three emotional attitudes common to family business patriarchs interfere with their ability to face the future. These attitudes form the core of a series of excuses or refusals to consider forming a Council and opening up decision-making to include others. They are deeply rooted, and must be considered the key obstacles to facing the future effectively:

Denial/Avoidance: It's hard to conceive of your own death or disability when you are healthy and vital. It's hard to take time for the future when the present demands attention. It seems easier to play the odds, and put things off. As a result, business owners don't learn about estate tax laws, make a will, develop successors, or think of "what-if" possibilities. Ignorance helps them deny the possibility of death, and postpone difficult choices about the future. When founders are in a state of denial, they don't look ahead. Since they don't think the problems exist, they get angry at people who say they do. When change, conflict, or crisis finally hits, it can be overwhelming because none of the groundwork has been laid.

Secrecy: Business owners often believe it will hurt other family members to talk about their desires or intentions, or they don't feel it is anyone else's business. They don't think they should share business information, that it is bad luck, or upsetting. Secrecy keeps heirs and managers off balance and fosters either withdrawal or obsessive attention to the patriarch's needs. It can play off one family member against the other, and it can cause them to manipulate one another. The result is that such owners' good intentions are often misunderstood, or create the opposite results.

Distrust: Owners may distrust the motives of advisors, or not know how to find the people they can really trust. They may be accustomed to keeping their own counsel, and doing things on their own. After all, they are entrepreneurs. They make assumptions like "All lawyers are crooks"; or "I can't talk about our affairs to anyone." They use distrust as an excuse not to listen to anyone, and to insulate their ideas and plans from scrutiny by others, including other family members.

All three of these underminers sow the evils they were trying to avoid. By sealing themselves off from reality and not letting others in, owners run the risk of losing vast fortunes, seeing their businesses decline, and the next generation ill prepared for leadership. In the vacuum, nobody in the family knows where he or she stands, and the situation can disintegrate into feuds, recriminations, and backbiting, with everyone trying to curry favor with the throne. The future of the business is threatened as its resiliency is lost, and good managers, inside and outside the family, bail out. In the end, the family does not realize its heritage.

Reflection Question

If you are the business and family leader, think of your own planning for your personal, family, and business future. Your first thought may be, "I've taken care of it," or "I don't need to get into that yet." These are all forms of resistance. Write a list of all the ways that you may avoid, deny, resist, or distrust planning for your future. For each reason write down some of the beneficial and negative results of that behavior. Then ask yourself if you might look at things differently and open up your family and business deliberations.

Because of these attitudes on the part of entrepreneurs, it is often the family heirs, spouses, or in-laws who first feel the need for the Council. They may be concerned or uncertain about the future, or they may want to know more about the business, or where they stand within it. They may be on the verge of making a decision about their personal future, and want to know what they can expect from the business. They may be concerned about a recent business decision and wonder whether it is proper to say something. Many times heirs have been working in the business, and wonder about the future plans of their parent/leader. They don't feel that can ask at work, and aren't sure it is right to bring up at home. So they avoid the issue. Sometimes they try to bring it up and get rebuffed.

The next step is critical. What do you do when you suggest a Council and get a negative response? When Dad resists, saying he doesn't think there is anything to discuss? Too many family members respond by withdrawing, assuming from the response that there is nothing they can do. Not so. At several family business conferences, I've run workshops on how members of the younger generation can influence the older generation to share information, power, and eventual ownership. I find that in most such situations, the younger person gives up much too quickly. It takes persistence to change old habits and attitudes.

In fact, if you want to initiate a Family Council, many strategies are open to you. One is to meet without the owner. One person, no matter how important, should not be allowed to keep a gathering from occurring. Everyone does not have to be there to get started, and if you wait for everybody, you may be short-circuiting your own future. The resisters can be invited to come as observers, or told that they are always welcome, and that what takes place will be shared. If the first meeting goes well, skeptics are usually willing to come to the second one.

A group of siblings of a large and complex family business with many trusts asked the father to initiate meetings so they could understand the trusts and their future. He declined, saying he was too busy. They met themselves, sharing their frustration. Then one daughter wondered if she could invite their lawyer. After all, she felt, he represented them too, and had said he was their advisor. He agreed to come to discuss the meaning of their various trusts. He came for a few meetings, and then they invited another advisor. After about six months of meetings, the father asked if he might come. They said fine, and he hardly remembered he had rejected their first invitation!

You need to act creatively to overcome the resistance of the single holdout. Often that person has concerns or fears about family gatherings that need to be taken into account. One spouse was adamantly opposed to family meetings. When asked about her reasons, she admitted that she was afraid that she would get criticized, and that the meeting would turn into an angry, unproductive argument. Her fears were realistic, and until adequate safeguards could be arrived at, she didn't want meetings.

Another way to get a commitment to the Council is to have other families that have created one share their experience. The best way to convince a resistant member of the older generation is to have a peer take him or her out to dinner and explain how the Council worked for the peer's family. It sometimes helps to enlist the aid of a consultant. At times I have helped a family have their first meetings simply by creating a safe environment, and being there to make sure things stayed on track. One person said I was her "security blanket."

The Initial Family Retreat

The best way to initiate the Council is away from home at a family retreat lasting a few days. Going away underscores the special meaning of the event, and gives family members a place away from everyday pressures and enough time to reflect on their thoughts and feelings. If you try to create a Council at an evening meeting, you run the risk of having volatile issues come up without time to reach resolution, which may be frustrating and upsetting.

Once family members are committed, scheduling the retreat is only the first step. As the convener, you need to do much more than just set a time. People want to know what will happen, and what they are expected to do. They will probably be somewhat anxious or concerned about what can be said, and the possibility of unresolvable conflict. The retreat should not be a presentation by an expert, nor simply a recitation of plans by Dad about the business. It is a participatory gathering. Each individual must prepare, and everybody needs a chance to work on the agenda and ground rules. The more interaction that occurs before the retreat, the more people will be committed to the retreat itself, and prepared to raise key issues.

A Family Council retreat starts with a planning group. Even though you are all a family, the Council is an organization, and the more clear information you can get from each person, the more effective the planning can be. If the family business consists of only a single family of parents and children, the planners can be the whole family. They draw up objectives, and gather information from other family members. They listen to concerns, and ask about issues that need to be addressed. Larger families send around a survey, and collect written responses from each person.

People feel more committed to a group when they feel that their concerns will be addressed, and that they have a say in the direction of the group. Therefore it is important that everyone participates in forming the Council. Otherwise, you run the risk of having something "come up" at the last minute which prevents key people from attending, or having people participate passively or distantly. From the start, the Council should not be perceived as a platform for a powerful family patriarch. In fact, it might be helpful to have the business leader not be the leader and convener of the Council retreat. Probably, the patriarch can be persuaded that he is too busy to lead the group, and some other person can take it on. Sometimes it is helpful for one of the least connected family members to become the convener, which brings him or her more into the family orbit.

Every family member over a certain age should participate. Children from 12 to 16 are often not included, but in my experience, they are often curious about the business and beginning to think about their future. Sometimes members from far away, or those who feel distant, are reluctant to participate. They may feel that the Council is an attempt to force them to be "closer." They need to be reassured that what is being asked for is only their caring and respectful participation in a forum to discuss common issues. If family members know they are meeting twice a year to discuss differences, sometimes incipient feuds or difficulties between two people can be avoided or limited.

Calling the first Council meeting often has the effect of "activating the family network." This means that, as the idea is proposed and family members recall their concerns, hurts, anger, and difficulties, they become both afraid of the power of the gathering, and also hopeful. Just calling a meeting gets the family to begin new behavior—talking to one another about shared concerns. Siblings call one another and get together. Everyone begins to talk about the issues that will come up in the meeting.

Early on in the planning process, the family needs to generate a list of issues, concerns, topics, and questions. They can be written on paper and put up for all to see. One method for setting an agenda is to put up the list of everyone's concerns, and then give everyone five votes for the important issues. They can "spend" their five votes on one topic, or spread them around. After everyone has voted, the topics and concerns will be prioritized. Some of the topics may be similar, and others may fit naturally together. From this list an agenda can be planned. The following exercise may be helpful in generating a list to vote on.

Achieving Business-Family Balance

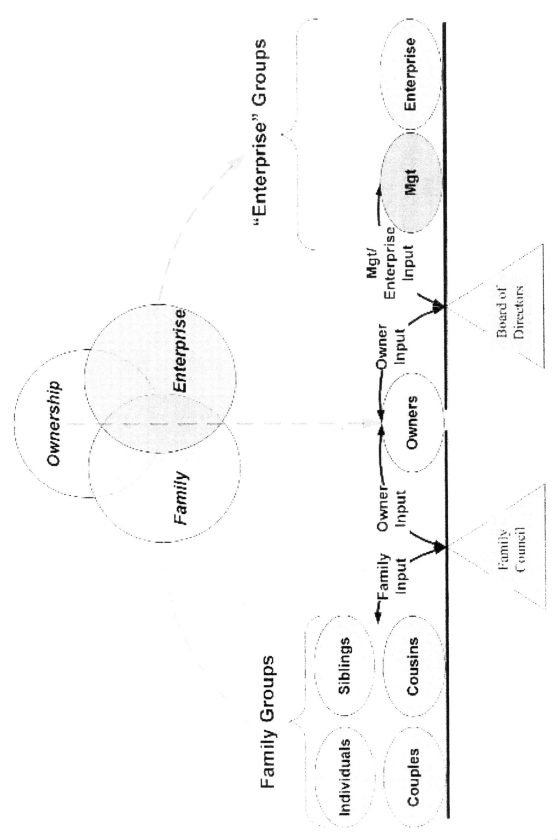

Life Cycles/
Development Stages

Enterprise

- Maturity
- Growth
- Expansion
- Survival
- Start up

Family

- Couples
- Family with children
- Launching young adults
- Family without children

Ownership

- Controlling Owner / Founder
- Parent-Offspring Partnership
- Sibling Partnership
- Cousin Consortium

Source: Gersick, Davis, Hampton, Lansberg, 1999

21

Family Council Focus Areas

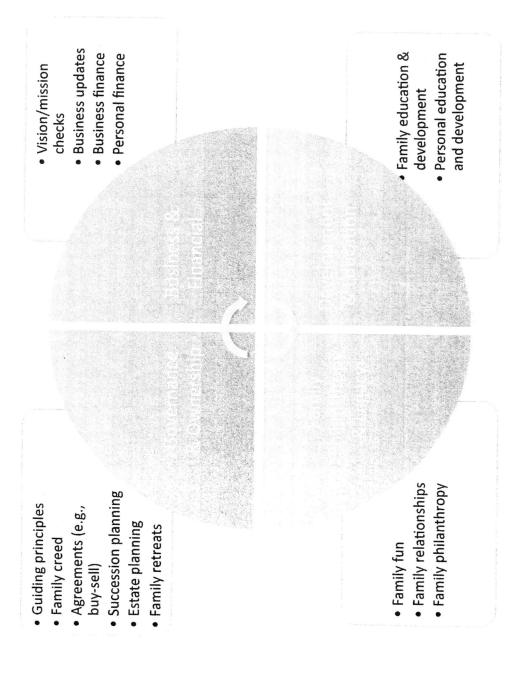

- Guiding principles
- Family creed
- Agreements (e.g., buy-sell)
- Succession planning
- Estate planning
- Family retreats

Governance & Ownership

- Vision/mission checks
- Business updates
- Business finance
- Personal finance

Business & Financial

- Family education & development
- Personal education and development

- Family fun
- Family relationships
- Family philanthropy

Source: Adapted from {Meghan Juday, Ideal Industries], Transitions West 2012.

27

95

"THOSE FAMILY BUSINESSES WHICH
GO ON FROM GENERATION TO
GENERATION, THOSE WHO ARE
SUCCESSFUL IN SURVIVING THE
INCREDIBLE ECONOMIC AND
SOCIAL CURRENTS, TYPICALLY HAVE
A FUNDAMENTAL CORE OF VALUES
THAT IN SOME WAY PASS THROUGH
THE GENERATIONS."

by Craig Aronoff

OPERATIONAL VALUES		LIFE VALUES	
Affection		Family	
Honesty		Love	
Loyalty		Health	
Courtesy		Happiness	
Autonomy		Self-worth	
Competency		Wisdom	
Knowledge		Fellowship	
Humor		Aesthetics	
Creativity		Community	
Order		Freedom	
Accountability		Pleasure	
Tolerance		Achievement	
Service		Wealth	
Fairness		Social Service	
Flexibility		Peace	
Discipline		Equality	
Forgiveness		Adventure	
Courage		Nature	
Reason		Power	
Drive		Spirituality	
Obedience		Fame	

(Prioritize by simply numbering each column 1 – 21)

Values are enduring beliefs that a certain way of behaving or certain life goals are personally or socially preferable to you. Think of the values you hold as the preferred way of behaving or our preferred-longer term goals. These values are referred to as Operational and Life Values. While Operational Values define the behavioral "means" by which you achieve your goals, Life Values define what those goals are.

Values do not exist independently, but rather in a complex system of Operational and Life Values. Consciously or unconsciously, your value system is the set of life priorities that govern all of your actions and determine all of your life goals.

A Family Council

What is it?

1. It is a platform for your voice to be heard
2. It is not a legal entity
3. Meets usually semi-annually
4. Addresses the emotional needs of the family

What does it do?

1. Creates the Family Creed/Code of Ethics, Guiding Principles and a Family Constitution, Family Employment Policies etc.
2. Gives the Vision of the Family Business
3. Addresses the Values of the Family vis a vis the Business
4. Creates Development and Mentoring programs for the Next Generation
5. Educates using case studies and readings to all family council members

Who should be on the Family Council?

1. All Family Members who work in the Family Business
2. Shareholders of the Family Business
3. Owners of the Family Business
4. In Laws or e they Out Laws?
5. All Family Members including children aged 15 and up

Board of Directors

Definition: A Board of Directors is a creature of law created by section 300 of the California Corporations Code. The Board has authority only to the extent the Corporation Code provides.

Purpose:
- The business and affairs of the corporation shall be managed and all corporate powers shall be exercised by or under the direction of the board. The board may delegate the management of the day-to-day operation of the corporation to a management company or other person provided that the business and the affairs of the corporation shall be managed and all corporate powers shall be exercised under the ultimate direction of the board.
- Election (and removal) of Officers (President, Treasurer, Secretary) – sometimes Vice Presidents.
- Guide "big picture" course of the company
  a. Business judgment. Stay informed
  b. Put family plan into practice
- Fiduciary duties
  c. In general: Do not treat shareholder or group of shareholders differently from other similarly situated shareholders.
  d. Loyalty – do not take corporate opportunities

Who Should Be On It?
- 1 Shareholder – 1 Director
- 2 Shareholders – 2 Directors
- More than 2 Shareholders – at least 3 Directors
- Shareholder(s) – Remember the fiduciary duty
- Industry Experts (Usually a paid position)
- Family Members
  - Under what circumstances?

Board of Advisors

Definition: A Board of Advisors is a group of people put together at the discretion of the CEO and/or board of directors to give advice on how to proceed as a company. There is no legal basis for having or not having a Board of Advisors.

Purpose:
- The Board of Advisors has no authority in electing or removing officers
  a. No authority to set corporate priorities
  b. No authority to make decisions about share holders
- Gives advice to the Board (or Management) – "Influence"
  c. If board takes advice, it must do so by taking action as board. "Authority"
- Only acts when asked to do so

Who Should Be On It?
- Trusted Advisors – Retired Lawyers, Accountants, etc.
- Industry Experts
  a. Advisors are often paid with either equity or cash

Appendix C

Sample Family Creed

familyhzconsulting.com

Carmen Bianchi Family Business Associates

Family Values:

1. **Honesty and Integrity**

   Our character must be unquestionable in all of our dealings. It is one thing that no one can take from us. To ignore this can harm our family name and our business. Teach our children this above all things.

2. **Ethical Behavior**

   We must always strive to do good and we must understand that we have only a short time to do it. We are not measured by what we have, but by who we are.

3. **Family**

   Family is what makes our business special. Our elders deserve our gratitude and respect for getting us here and our youth deserve our attention to their growth and development, as they will take our place in this business. Treat all family members with respect. Do not fight. Disagreements should be worked out privately with the result fully supported by all involved. Recognize our differences as a strength that provides a greater variety of ideas and perspectives to our business. Don't hesitate to communicate when there is a problem. Because we care about our family, we must work to make our world, our community, and our business better for the next generation.

10

4. Responsibility

To live a full life, we must accomplish many things. There is no short cut to success. We must always seek new challenges and new education. In this way, we gain the experience that prepares us to contribute more. For our accomplishments to have any flavor they cannot be delegated; they must be our own. In our family and in our business, we have to do what we promise and take responsibility for our actions and their outcomes.

5. Fairness

We must encourage and reward those who contribute and make a difference, not simply reward by birthright. Put the right person in the right job. They will contribute more and toil less. This sense of fairness needs to be extended especially to non-family employees. They must know that they will be given every opportunity to succeed and contribute to the success of the business.

6. Fun

We are a family. To be successful, we have to want to be together and enjoy each other's company. It is important to maintain balance in our lives. Our families deserve our love and attention and, in the end, it is they who will care for us more than anyone we have known in our business.

Family Guiding Principles:

1. Qualifications:

Family members who meet the qualifications required for a position at the company are to be given the opportunity to apply for and interview for any job opening. A job will not be created specifically for a family member. The open job position is not guaranteed for a family member and other more qualified candidates unless it is for the good of the business as determined by the Board of Directors.

2. Compensation:

Pay will be determined by experience, skills, performance and level of responsibility of the family member. Each job will be paid in accordance with other jobs with similar title, level or responsibility.

11

3. **Leadership:**

For the business to thrive, the best talent should be brought into the business. Leadership and responsibility is earned. Title/Office is earned through performance and experience. The office and title of President or any other office is not guaranteed to family members. Continuing education for company leadership and management is necessary to keep the mind sharp, provide new ideas, and ultimately benefit the business.

4. **Experience/Education:**

Being able to bring new ideas and innovations to the family business adds credibility and value to a family member. Therefore, outside experience/education according to the specific job description in one of our industries is more important than years of service in the family business. It is essential that each family member views work as a slow accumulation of a large body of knowledge. Knowledge needed to benefit the company cannot come quickly or easily. It must be gained slowly over the years through experience. If a family member wishes to work in the management of the family business, he/she must work outside the business for a minimum of three years or be promoted from within This provides credibility to the family member by showing that they are promotable in their field and successful in their own right. Family members may leave the business to gain experience or education elsewhere knowing that they may return to the business later.

5. **Work Ethic:**

A strong desire to work hard, add value and be a team player is critical for every company employee, especially family. Family members must also personify the family values and set a good example, all while practicing humility and respect to their supervisors and co-workers. Family members should strive to be the best in order to motivate others. Family members not adhering to the policies and procedures required at the company will be subject to the same disciplinary actions as any other employee.

6. **Mentoring:**

The mentoring program is required for all family members entering the business. Family members will be assigned mentors within the business who will provide guidance and support to the mentee as well as provide feedback to their supervisor.

12

7. **Respect:**

Respect the people you work with, their job position, as well as the family name. Keep true to the family values as stated in the Creed. Do not use the family name as a way of gaining advantage.

8. **Organizational Boundaries:**

Honor your boss and respect organizational boundaries. Family members are not to influence or interfere on behalf of other family members across organizational boundaries. Seeking advice of counsel from family members is acceptable. Family members working in the business will solve organizational issues and problems within their own departments/organization and through the regular chain of command.

9. **Contracted Services:**

When a family member is to provide contracted services for the business, the executive with budget responsibility for that service or function will be responsible for initiating contact and managing the relationship throughout the life of the agreement. This is to be an arms-length agreement according to the policies set by the Board of Directors.

10. **Departure and Termination:**

Family members who wish to exit the family business may do so according to the exit rules/codes for any employee of the family business. Should the family member due to performance evaluations be required by the Board of Directors and/or senior management to exit the family business, this will be according to the rules and regulations for any employee in a similar situation. This is a business first company and all family members employed by the company will be treated as employees with no preferential treatment. Should the family members' desire be to continue to be employed by the family business in a different capacity other than the current one, then only if that position is available can such family member apply for the position. Positions for family members will not be "invented" unless agreed upon by the Board of Directors as being necessary to the family business.

The Ten Commandments
of a Successful Family Business

1. Do only what you do best, let others do the rest.

2. Always think of your non-family member employees as who they can be, not what they can do.

3. Read often, so you don't get dull-minded. With your family at home, discuss your readings and not your business.

4. Always treat your customers so you would be glad to see them in church tomorrow.

5. Have your family help you discover at least five ways to define success that do not include making money. Use those definitions as your business and family goals and values.

6. Remember that you can never give enough to the community that supports your business.

7. Teach your children to teach, but only after they have learned.

8. Help your employees to celebrate what is important to them.

9. Always practice humility. The only room for pride in your business is your employees' pride in their work.

10. Do not go to sleep at night without thanking God you are in America and telling every family member you love them.

Elvira LoConte-Marchigiano (1888-1957)

THE CENTER FOR FAMILY BUSINESS

University Services Institute

TWELVE COMMANDMENTS
for the
BUSINESS OWNER

1. Thou Shalt Share Thy Dream With Thy Family.

2. Thou Shalt Inform Thy Managers and Employees, "This Company Will Continue Forever."

3. Thou Shalt Develop a Workable Organization and Make It Visible on a Chart.

4. Thou Shalt Continue to Improve Thy Management Knowledge, That of Thy Managers and That of Thy Family.

5. Thou Shalt Institute an Orthodox Accounting System and Make Available the Data Therefrom to Thy Managers, Advisors, and Directors.

6. Thou Shalt Develop a Council of Competent Advisors.

7. Thou Shalt Submit Thyself to the Review of a Board of Competent Outside Directors.

8. Thou Shalt Choose Thy Successor(s).

9. Thou Shalt Be Responsible That Thy Successor(s) be Well Taught.

10. Thou Shalt Retire and Install Thy Successor(s) With Thy Powers Within Thy Lifetime.

11. Thou Canst Not Take It With Thee - So Settle Thy Estate Plans - Now.

12. Thou Shalt Apportion Thy Time to See That These Commandments Be Kept.

LÉON A. DANCO, Ph.D.
President, The Center for Family Business

THE CENTER FOR FAMILY BUSINESS • P.O. Box 24219 • Cleveland, Ohio 44124 • Dial 216/442-0800

KIKKOMAN'S MOGI FAMILY CREED

Get a bottle of Kikkoman Soy Sauce and look at the label—you'll see the date 1630. That's when the Mogi family began the business, and they've owned and operated it for 17 generations since.

Current CEO Yuzaburo Mogi recently traveled from Japan to speak to Loyola University Chicago's Family Business Forum and was guest speaker at the Georgia Family Business of the Year Awards luncheon. As part of his presentation, he shared his family's creed, written over a century ago and still used to guide the family and its business. Here it is, translated from Japanese:

Article I:

All family members desire peace. Never fight, and always respect each other. Ensure progress in business and the perpetuation of family prosperity.

Article II:

Loving God and Buddha is the source of all virtue. Keeping faith leads to a peaceful mind.

Article III:

All family members should be polite to each other. If the master is not polite, the others will not follow. Sin is the result of being impolite. Families—young and old, masters and workers—govern themselves by politeness; then peace will be brought of their own accord.

Article IV:

Virtue is the cause, fortune the effect. Never mistake the cause for the effect. Never judge people on whether they are rich or not.

Article V:

Keep strict discipline. Demand diligence. Preserve order—young and old, master and workers.

Article VI:

Business depends on people. Do not make appointments or dismissals using personal prejudices. Put the right man in the right place. Loving men who do what they should bring peace to their minds.

Article VII:

Education of the children is our responsibility to the nation. Train the body and mind with moral, intellectual and physical education.

Article VIII:

Approach all living beings with love. Love is fundamental to human beings and the source of a life worth living. Words are the door to fortune and misfortune. A foul tongue hurts oneself and others. A kind tongue keeps everything peaceful. Be careful in every word you speak.

Article IX:

Keep humbleness and diligence, which have been handed down over the years from our forefathers. Make every effort to do as much as you can.

Article X:

True earning comes from the labor of sweat. Speculation is not the best road to follow. Don't do business by taking advantage of another's weakness.

Article XI:

Competition is an important factor in progress, but avoid extreme or unreasonable competition. Strive to prosper together with the public.

Article XII:

Make success or failure clear, judge fairly punishment and reward. Never fail to reward meritorious service, and don't allow a mistake to go unpunished.

Article XIII:

Consult with family members when starting a new business. Never try to do anything alone. Always appreciate any profit made by your family.

Article XIV:

Don't carelessly fall into debt. Don't recklessly be a guarantor of liability. Don't lend money with the purpose of gaining interest, because you are not a bank.

Article XV:

Save money from your earnings and give to society as much as you can. But never ask for a reward nor think highly of yourself.

Article XVI:

Don't decide important affairs by yourself. Always consult with the people concerned before making a decision. Then employees will have a positive attitude in their work.

Ed Azar, Sr.

Some Advice to Family Businesses

All family businesses are fragile and, as such, should be marked "Fragile – Handle With Professional Care." Family members must practice the basic disciplines and create the same organizational structure as any company, private or public. The following are a few, and are certainly not all, of the things a family business should do.

1. Elect an active and empowered board of directors to oversee management's performance. Certainly outsiders are desirable. They bring a fresh perspective.

2. Elect the most qualified family member to act as CEO, be he chairman or president.

3. Develop and update your strategic plan, including identifying a successor CEO in the event of a premature death or retirement.

4. Create, communicate, advise and coordinate innovative strategies for the company's continued success. This can be done through operating committees, executive committees and meetings of the board of directors.

5. Establish standards and budgets and respect the commitment. Do what you say you will do.

6. Family members should set examples for the rest of the work force and their colleagues. Be energetic, be responsible and enthusiastic, for after all, we are responsible for establishing company standards.

7. Continued education is a must, especially in today's environment. The rate of change in all technology demands our attention. As we move from protective market to open market, we must have the knowledge, the understanding and the ability to move quickly and confidently.

8. Keep wives, husbands and egos in check. Well meaning spouses can irreparably influence and damage family business relationships. They are a powerful force in our lives and must be reckoned with. Establish boundaries and guard them well.

9. Be ethical and moral in your dealings. If there is a hint of dishonesty, you run the risk of losing the respect of customers, suppliers and employees and even family members.

10. Expect and earn employee loyalty. This is so important! Give me a loyal employee anytime over a marginally more competent one. You simply must have people you can depend upon and trust. They guard your rear and flank.

11. Seek counsel on family problems. I did and it paid terrific dividends. There was a time counseling carried with it a stigma – that's no longer true. It's a fool who doesn't seek professional help and advice when needed.

12. Create an environment free of discrimination, favoritism and to whatever extent possible, nepotism, so that non-family members can expect promotions when they've earned them.

13. Insulate the family troublemaker from the rest of the work force until he or she settles down. If the turmoil continues, perhaps the only solution is to terminate. Tough, but necessary. There is no business that can endure the punishment resulting from thoughtless, senseless corporate bashing.

14. Be patient with slow family developers. As long as there is gradual and measurable improvement, nurture and encourage his or her continued development. As a rule, family players care more about the success of the company than non-family employees. After all, their capital is at risk.

15. Heated family discussions should take place only in private and behind closed doors. Open arguments tend to polarize and confuse the work force.

16. After all else fails, make certain that you have a buy and sell agreement in place to protect your sanity and to protect the company and its employees.

17. Finally, be sensitive and realistic with respect to the company's future. A favorite western ballad of mine is one sung by Kenny Rogers. The title is "The Gambler." The advice of the gambler to the stranger is "There's a time to hold them and a time to fold them and a time to walk away and a time to run." Eventually, every CEO must face the painful but inevitable decision of succession – "hold them" or liquidation, or sale, or merger, "fold them." The decision is never easy, nor is it always right, nor is it ever a win-win proposition. There will forever be winners and losers, the satisfied and the dissatisfied.

We're only human, so once you've made a decision, don't look back – you've done the best you could!

5

Family Council Roles:
Chief Emotional Officer (CEO)

Choose someone:

- With a high degree of emotional maturity
- With a healthy ego and self-confidence
- Who is trustworthy and maintains boundaries
- Who respects family traditions and values
- Who understands the difference between being in the middle of things rather than the center of things
- Who will step up and speak out when irregularities occur
- Who is a skilled communicator
- Who can tailor their approach to a given situation

Source: Leslie Mayer, Family Business, Summer 2008

Family Council Roles & Responsibilities

Chief Emotional Officer: Responsible for creating family council agenda, coordinating meeting agenda with facilitator

Historian : Responsible for creating a video and/or photo archive of family council meetings, writing family business history, and recording ethical wills

Secretary/Treasurer: Responsible for recording minutes of the family council meetings. Work with Social Director on travel expenses. Record milestone events for the historian.

Social Director : Responsible for choosing dates, locations, and activities for family council meetings

26

Sonnenfeld and Spence
Parting Patriarchs

Four Retirement Styles:

1. Monarch

2. General

3. Governor

4. Ambassador

Sonnenfeld and Spence
Parting Patriarchs

Entrepreneurs and Top Executives suffer from a *Heroic Self-Concept*, characterized by:

- strong identification with leadership stature
- unrelenting quest for immortal contribution

The phases of a successful hero's life:

1. Separation from society
2. Continual trials and challenges which are met with success
3. Triumphant reintegration into society

Sonnenfeld and Spence
Parting Patriarchs

Barriers to Exiting:

Heroic Stature:
identification with the leadership role and stature; with the unique position of power, with the separation from others.

■ This identification and problems associated with it are heightened in the family firm, due to dual leadership roles of CEO and father.

■ To lose this identity in retirement is very frightening

Sonnenfeld and Spence
Parting Patriarchs

Barriers to Exit:

Heroic Mission:

sense that one is uniquely qualified to fulfill the leader role and accomplish the mission

- Departing leaders often fear they are leaving before they attain their highest goals
- Even with a good record, they might wonder what more they could accomplish if only they had time
- Since they've always been in control of their careers, this lack of control is very frightening

Sonnenfeld and Spence
Parting Patriarchs

Monarchs

- typical of founding entrepreneurs
- often command smaller firms and retain close strategic control
- they control their board of directors
- they created long-term growth and success
- have difficulty with both barriers
- are reluctant to consider life after retirement; have not developed the concept of a future, separate identity
- see retirement as being way too early

Sonnenfeld and Spence
Parting Patriarchs

Monarchs

- in late career, they are unable to top past accomplishments, and want to stay for one more big one

- they wish their career would never end

In summary, Monarchs experience a troubled, forced exit, failing to master either heroic stature or heroic mission

- enmeshed in company, has fear
- identifies w/ company, always executive role
- "if" im going to die.

Departure Styles
(Phase 2)

MONARCHS

- most troubled by heroic stature and mission barriers

- must be forced out of office

- threatened and bitter over loss of power

Succession Planning for Monarchs
(Phase 2)

- Influence by showing how recognition, control, and power can be satisfied in other areas

- Use force only as a last resort

- Expose to other exit patterns — help perceive choices

- Use other CEOs as examples

Sonnenfeld and Spence
Parting Patriarchs

Generals

- manage larger firms
- still closely identify with firm
- are less successful at long-term growth and vision, and therefore
- retain less strategic control
- they often had increased sales and market share during last years, but failed to develop long-term interests
- often, they are ousted for their ineffectiveness
- they have not planned for retirement, and still identify with the leadership role

Sonnenfeld and Spence
Parting Patriarchs

Generals

■ in fact, may plot to come back

In summary, Generals show least mastery of heroic stature and little concern for heroic mission; they are bitter and angry about having their identify stripped away, but less concerned about performance and contribution

Departure Styles
(Phase 2)

GENERALS

- heroic stature a major issue

- must be forced out, but plan their return to rescue the company

- like to exit with a flourish

- very threatened by loss of status and power

Succession Planning for Generals
(Phase 2)

- Use same techniques as for monarchs

- Develop clear, measurable performance standards for successor

- Decide in advance how much change from tradition will be acceptable under the new leader

Sonnenfeld and Spence
Parting Patriarchs

Governors

- manage the largest companies

- serve the shortest terms

- work in environments where there are formal procedures for succession

- demonstrate consistent, high performance which is increased further in last couple years of office

- leave with energy and enthusiasm – enthusiasm to make new contributions in the world of business

- don't regret loss of leader stature, but have the most difficulty with mastering heroic mission

Departure Styles
(Phase 2)

GOVERNORS

- yearn for a new heroic mission, least concerned with heroic stature

- when departing, make a clean break

- eager to exit for new opportunities

Succession Planning for Governors
(Phase 2)

- Use same techniques as for ambassadors

- Have them work very closely with their successors

- Provide opportunities to be helpful

- Use to pass on the traditions, values, and beliefs of the firm

Sonnenfeld and Spence

Parting Patriarchs

Ambassadors:

- healthiest departure
- manage larger firms
- they performed steadily; preserved and maintained a growth pattern
- they leave willingly and gracefully
- they maintain contact as advisory
- they are satisfied with retirement and with their past contributions to business
- they make the transition to other interests and roles

Departure Styles
(Phase 2)

AMBASSADORS

- least troubled by heroic stature and mission barriers

- leave willingly and gracefully

- usually have many outside interests

Succession Planning for Ambassadors
(Phase 2)

- Link into their needs for acceptance

- Let them remain with the firm as advisors

- Realize that ambassadors

  - usually respond to reason and to sound business advice

  - are most receptive to discussing succession as an issue

  - consider keeping connected crucial

Personal Attributes and Departure Styles of "Retiring Heroes"

PERSONAL ATTRIBUTES:	Monarch	General	Ambassador	Governor
Identification	Company - enmeshed - likes to live legacy - don't give up	Chief Executive Role - doesn't care about legacy	Company - usually made chairman of board	Career
Perceived Trauma	Loss of Influence	Loss of Mission, Respect - fear of loss of status/power	None, Enjoy New Role	None, Move on to New Venture
Reaction to Successors	Undermine Them	Question Their Competence; Fight Them	Support & Mentor Them	Build Strong Successors; Then Leave Them Alone
Downside of Retirement	Loss of Self Esteem	Boredom; Desire to Return	None; Change in Role	None; Change Careers
Outside Interests	Some, but Not Satisfying	Few and Not Satisfying	Many; Stay With Company as Elder Statesman	Many; Can Become New Venture
Legacy	Built the Company	Hero	Successful Career & Mentor - nice transition	Multiple Successes in Career

W:Frether

CarmenBianchi
14758 Caminito Punta Arenas
Del Mar, California 92014
Phone: 858-793-2445 Fax: 858- 777-3556
Email carmbianchi@yahoo.com

Sonnenfeld and Spence

A 68 year old successful CEO/Founder has prepared and put his daughter JoAnn aged 39, through many years of development as the successor to the business. She has an MBA is extremely talented and has a hands on working knowledge of all the different areas of the business.

1. **What do you see as the major obstacle for succession?**
    a. **For the Retiring Hero**
    b. **For the Aspiring Hero**

2. **What recommendations would you make to facilitate the succession?** Get him gone so he stops undermining person taking over. put him on board of directors in other company. And other interests.

multipliers (Book)

Family Business Management

Guidelines for creating a Genogram

Please refer to the handouts/templates when constructing your genogram

Each individual student is expected to go back at least 3 generations if not more. Ideally 5 generations would be best.

The student-learning objective of doing a genogram is to:

a. Inform us of family names, relationships, birth order, and linear descendants.
b. Capture events such as immigration, marriage, divorce, and separation.
c. Patterns and trends such as illness, alcoholism.
d. Educational patterns, schoolteachers, scientists, inventors etc.
e. Critical incidents, sudden deaths, conflictual relationships
f. Cultural differences
g. Knowledge of how to use the genogram as a tool for assessing the structural process elements of a family system
h. Skills in assessing family dynamics and how they impact the family business
i. Identify the family's psychological relationships and communication patterns

Genograms have helped therapists and family business consultants better "read" and understand the influences of the family relationships. How families relate to one another, how they communicate with each other and how Bowen Theory identifies and influences these relationships by identifying triangulation, sibling rivalry and birth order.

Be as innovative as possible, include pictures, historical data, dates ages etc.. When presenting makes sure that the genogram is readable to the audience (your classmates) especially if it is in PowerPoint format.
Remember that some of the conversations you will have with family members may be sensitive in nature. Be sensitive to these conversations and discussions and ask permission to share the information. Some information may differ; it is not necessary to disclose what someone else said unless you again have his or her permission. This is an opportunity to reach out and speak to family members that perhaps you have not conversed with in a while. We ask all class members to keep what is disclosed in class as confidential.

This exercise is fun and at the same time extremely informative. I hope you enjoy creating the genogram as much as we will `enjoy sharing it with you.

Genogram Symbols

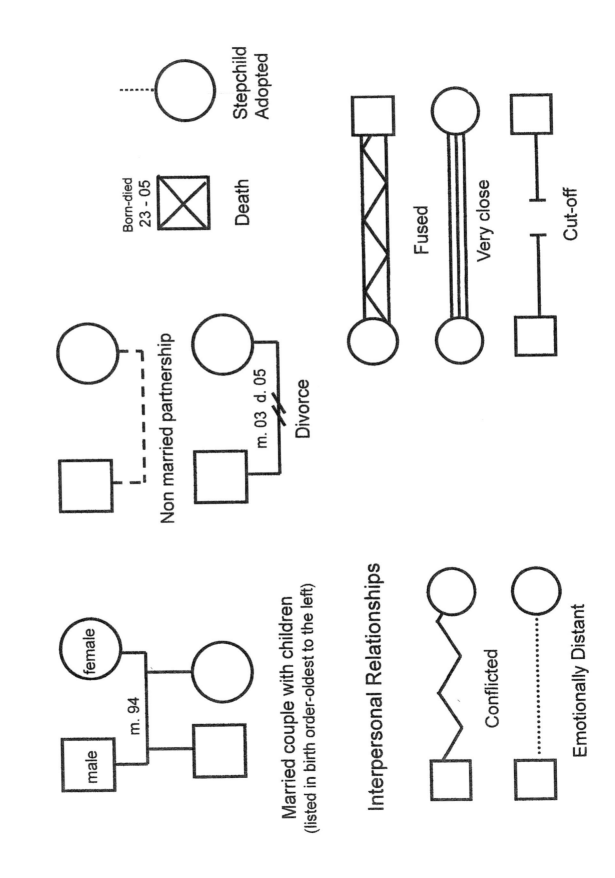

Stepchild
Adopted

Born-died
23 - 05
Death

Non married partnership

m. 03 d. 05
Divorce

Fused

Very close

Cut-off

female
male
m. 94

Married couple with children
(listed in birth order-oldest to the left)

Interpersonal Relationships

Conflicted

Emotionally Distant

GENOGRAM

A complete genogram should include:

1. Names and ages of all family members.
2. Exact dates of birth, marriage, separation, divorce, death, and other significant life events. Note coincidences.
3. Notations, with dates, about occupation, places of residence, illness, and changes in life course, on the genogram itself.
4. Information on three or more generations.

Key to Important Symbols:

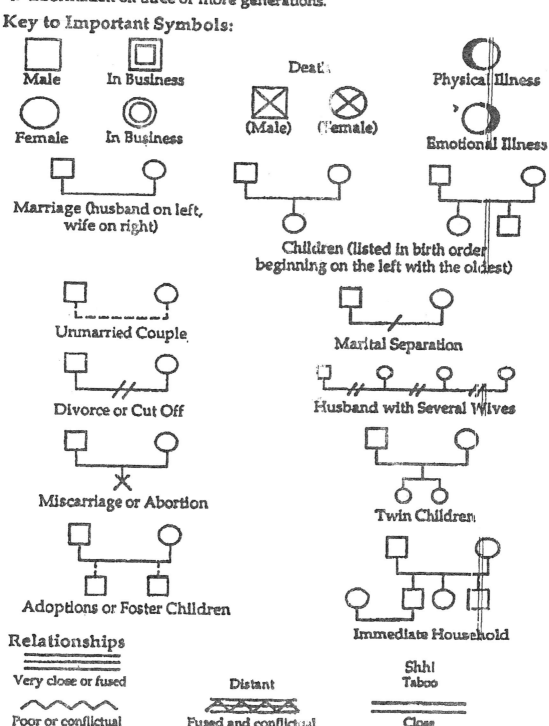

Male   In Business

Female   In Business

Death

(Male)   (Female)

Physical Illness

Emotional Illness

Marriage (husband on left, wife on right)

Children (listed in birth order beginning on the left with the oldest)

Unmarried Couple

Marital Separation

Divorce or Cut Off

Husband with Several Wives

Miscarriage or Abortion

Twin Children

Adoptions or Foster Children

Immediate Household

Relationships

Very close or fused

Poor or conflictual

Distant

Fused and conflictual

Shhh!
Taboo

Close

Appendix A

SYMBOLS FOR MAKING GENOGRAMS

The symbols and conventions here are commonly used and widely recognized, but if you find them inconvenient or if you need addtional ones, be creative.

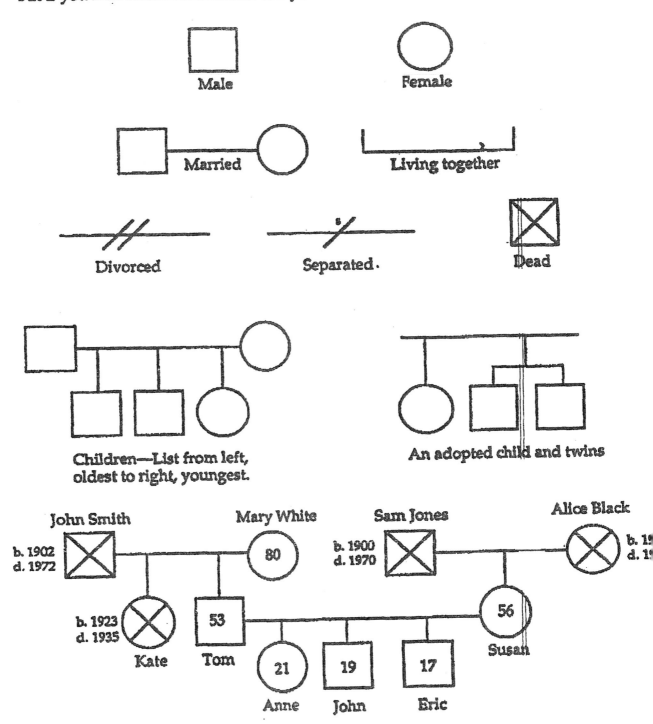

Male

Female

Married

Living together

Divorced

Separated.

Dead

Children—List from left, oldest to right, youngest.

An adopted child and twins

John Smith
b. 1902
d. 1972

Mary White
80

Sam Jones
b. 1900
d. 1970

Alice Black
b. 19
d. 19

Kate
b. 1923
d. 1935

Tom
53

Susan
56

Anne
21

John
19

Eric
17

Precista Tools AG (A)

April 30, 1986

Dear Mami and Papi:

Before I leave again for the United States, I think that I have to write to you. Papi asked me to let him know what my decisions are concerning my employment with Precista. He set the deadline.

I have decided to leave the company.

After a long period of thinking, I came to the conclusion that my attitude, my inner beliefs, and how the company should be managed to achieve its set goals are all basically different from the ideas that Papi has. Peace in our family has the highest priority, and I'm convinced that this step I take will keep peace and that you will understand my feeling and wish.

After my return from the United States, I will write to the Board and give formal notice. You can be assured, I promise, that I will stay with Precista until you have found a new solution. I still feel very responsible for the future of the company.

Now that I have made the decision—written down the words—I feel myself free, and I'm looking forward to a new environment in which I will be able to develop myself again. I hope that you will take me just as I am. I would just like to be a happy, content family member—nothing else.

With all my love,
Yours, Greta

A former OPM (Owner President Management Program) participant and Professor Louis B. Barnes wrote this case as a basis for class discussion rather than to illustrate either effective or ineffective handling of an administrative situation.

1

Background

Precista Tools A.G. was founded in Glarus, Switzerland, just after World War II by Franz Huebel who was born in 1913. Mr. Huebel and his wife, Sophie, were running a small international trading company out of Glarus. As Mr. Huebel said of Precista's origins:

> At the time we started the business, we had little money, a great deal of credit, a lot of ideas, and the will to make more money and work hard at it. But Precista could only become and stay leaders in the precision tool field if we were able to invest more money in product development than the average company could.

In order to raise money for product development, the Huebels poured the profits from the trading business into developing specialized precision tools for export out of the new business. By 1985, the company had 100 employees and 60 sales representatives throughout the world. Mr. Huebel had developed excellent marketing contacts in other countries where Precista became known for its sophisticated and well-engineered special-purpose precision tools. Precista became very successful and was still fully owned and tightly controlled by Franz Huebel.

On a personal level, Mr. and Mrs. Huebel had four children—three daughters and a son. Mrs. Huebel continued to work in company management, while a grandmother took care of the children. As one of them said: "Mother always played the mother role in the company and did whatever our father told her to do." Mr. Huebel, meanwhile, encouraged their son Peter—the third child—to come into the business when he grew up. In 1975, however, at age 25, Peter decided to seek a masters degree in engineering and not to enter the business. Among other things, Peter did not want to work for his father. However, the youngest daughter, Greta, did join the firm shortly after that as her father's assistant after graduating from college with an economics major. She not only worked with Mr. Huebel in Glarus but often accompanied him on sales trips to foreign countries. The two oldest daughters, both married, expressed no interest in becoming part of the company. Mr. Huebel seemed to value Greta's help, even giving her a Porsche convertible one year as a birthday present.

In 1980, Mr. Huebel had a serious heart attack and had to have triple by-pass surgery. After a three-month recovery, Mr. Huebel returned to the business, but his board of directors, particularly Dr. Riegel, a lawyer, tried to convince Mr. Huebel that he needed help in running the company. This was not the first time that Mr. Huebel had tried to bring in executive assistance. On three previous occasions, the effort had not worked out. Mr. Huebel also tried to interest Peter again in joining the company, but Peter was still involved in his engineering studies.

This time, the other members of the board—Dr. Hausman, an economist consultant, Mrs. Huebel, and Greta Huebel—joined Dr. Riegel in putting pressure on Mr. Huebel. They not only wanted to hire a new general manager but they also wanted to reorganize the company so that Mr. Huebel was less directly involved in detailed operations. Mr. Huebel eventually agreed.

Consequently, a professional general manager—Mr. Paul Schmeed—was hired. Mr. Schmeed came to work in March of 1983 after being employed in a large technical products firm. Mr. Schmeed was an engineer with considerable international management experience. Greta Huebel, then aged 30, was put in charge of Finance and Administration, along with Dr. Riegel's advice that "it is important for a family business to have a family member in charge of the finances, but you know that for all the rest of the business, we need a man who has technical training."

After that, Mr. Huebel stayed out of day-to-day management more. He would often come to work about 10:00 A.M. Later in the day he often walked around talking with engineers in the product development area. However, he also continued to read the minutes of all meetings and received reports from Greta at least once a week. Board of Directors meetings were held in Mr. Huebel's weekend chalet, but only after his daughter and Paul Schmeed had carefully gone over the agenda with him. Mr. Huebel would also attend one or two informal luncheons each week with his

2

managers or engineers. He would often invite the chief engineer to his office, and the two would work out major product decisions informally.

The arrangement worked fairly well for awhile. But then Mr. Huebel and Mr. Schmeed began to have disagreements. Mr. Huebel felt that Mr. Schmeed was interfering too much in some areas of product development. On one occasion, Mr. Huebel encountered a new engineer who was working on one of Mr. Huebel's favorite products. The engineer was making changes in the design which he said had come from the general manager. There were other similar incidents. By the fall of 1985, Mr. Huebel had decided that Paul Schmeed was not competent.

The Board Meeting of November 24th

At the November 24th board meeting Mr. Huebel proposed that Paul Schmeed be removed from his job. Excerpts from minutes of the board meeting are shown in **Exhibit 1**. At the same meeting, the board had a long discussion about two new organization plans. Neither involved hiring a new general manager. One plan set up a management committee of three functional department heads reporting to Mr. Huebel. The three departments were technical, finance/administration, and sales /marketing. The second plan divided the business into two major areas: commercial and technical. Greta Huebel would be made managing director of the commercial area, and Dr. Klaus Olander, the chief engineer, would be managing director of the technical area. The board adopted the second proposal by a four-to-one vote, with only Dr. Riegel, the lawyer, opposing the new plan. Dr. Riegel explained that his vote was not so much a vote against the plan as it was to call attention to its two major weaknesses that he saw being exacerbated by the second option. One concern was over whether the chief engineer, Dr. Olander, could take on new production technology and administrative duties effectively. Dr. Riegel said that "at this point, some production technology changes have to be made, and I doubt that Dr. Olander will be able to make them. I also question whether the production manager can help him."

Dr. Riegel's second concern related to the new reporting relationship of marketing and sales. They had previously been a separate department reporting to the general manager. Under the reorganization, they now reported to Greta Huebel. Dr. Riegel worried about this because "Precista needs a professional in that position who has a degree in engineering and who has done extensive course work in sales and marketing. Only if these two major points are covered will this new organization proposal be useful. As it currently stands, there is too big a gap between any experienced generalist and middle management."

Family Competition

In December 1985, Peter Huebel, now 35, graduated from the university with a masters degree in mechanical engineering. Although he and Greta had been close as children, they had grown apart in recent years as their lives and interests had taken separate paths. Earlier that year, Peter had done a school project at Precista on software optimization for one of the new electronic tool projects. He had satisfied the course requirements, but promised to come back and do more work on the company project in January and February of 1986. According to Greta:

> At the end of February, I was going to go on a one-week skiing vacation. Peter had finished his work and was going to take a one-month holiday. I left on a Thursday night, and on Friday my father signed an employment contract with my brother. When I came back, I knew that my father had a hard time telling me about it, but when he did, I asked him why he didn't talk about it before. He said, "I don't have to ask you about anything. It's my business and I run it the way I want to run it." He had never done anything like that before. During that same week I was gone, he had scheduled a meeting with some tax accountants, even though I was in charge of finances. I made special arrangements to come back from skiing for a day and

called him to say so. His reply was, "Well, if you really want to, but we've held these meetings for 40 years without you. Don't think that we can't do it alone."

It was like he really wanted to hurt me, which was entirely new. I couldn't understand this after all of those years when we had been so close together when there had been nothing that he didn't tell me. It had been such an open relationship. I think that it was partly because, for my father, Peter's joining the company was like a dream fulfilled. Not only did he now have a son for a successor, but it was a son who had a graduate degree—something my father never had. It was like a second life for him, even though his health was getting worse.

Some of the problems had nothing to do with the fact that I am a woman. It was a combination of things. It was being young, being a daughter, being a nonengineer, and being a woman. So some of these things would have happened anyway. When you're in the position that I was in—number two or number three in the company for 10 years—then when you get into your father's shadow, you're competing with him. Until 1986, I wasn't really competing with my father but from the time he made me managing director, I was competing—not from my side, but from his.

But being a woman did make a difference, and I talked with Peter about this. We both agreed that when it came down to making decisions, tradition said that leaders should be men. Also by tradition, if you have an only son—no matter how many daughters there are—then the man should be the one who takes charge. That was very deeply ingrained, not only with my father but with Dr. Riegel and Dr. Olander. It was even what my older sisters expected. My father started talking with them about the business, something he'd never done before. He was trying to turn them against me—telling them how I was trying to run the company differently. I think that it will take a long time before that will change.

Also in Switzerland, it's expected that you can only be head manager of a company like that if you're over 50. You can't be a young manager. You're too young. How could you be a leader at only 33 or 34. It's not possible.

Greta also felt that her problems were made worse because some employees felt that a high-tech company had to be managed by a technical person. In addition, she tried to get the sales people to become more marketing-oriented by developing market information and new product ideas as well as selling products. That was a change at Precista where marketing traditionally tried to sell whatever the technical department designed and produced. Greta went on to say:

My father was a pioneer in the industry, and he didn't want to give up control. I came in and wanted to make decisions too, but he wanted to be in charge and directly involved in the daily business. He became very angry when he read the minutes of those sales meetings, because he wanted to be the one to decide which products were created. When that happened a lot of people in the company became insecure, because they didn't know who was supposed to be doing what or who was the leader.

The Board Meeting of April 11

At 4:00 P.M. on April 10th, 1986, the day before the combined board meeting and annual meeting, Mr. Huebel called Greta into his office and said that he didn't agree with the agenda items that she had proposed. Greta wanted the board to reconsider its November 24th, 1985, reorganization decision. She wanted to bring in a new finance and administration manager who would also be on the management committee so that she could devote more time to sales and marketing. Mr. Huebel told his daughter that if she didn't like the way he was running the company, maybe she should go out and look for another job. Greta reported:

> That's when I changed. I knew my agenda proposals would stir controversy, but I also knew that I couldn't let him get to me that way. I was trying to get someone new onto the management committee who would be more on my side, because I wasn't getting any support from the technical people. Even when any of the other managers agreed with me, they were under enormous pressure to go along with him. And I wasn't going to let him pressure me. So I said that I'd always considered us a partnership, but that if that's the way he felt, that he should say so the next day at the board meeting. Then the others could hear his words and know that he didn't want to put up with me. I also asked—and I know it sounded a little bit arrogant—Is that all you want to tell me? He was shocked. I didn't argue. I just said, if that's what you want, just repeat it tomorrow at the meeting, and that made him mad. Then, I left his office.

> When I got outside, though, I just couldn't believe what he had said. I was mad and sad and hurt.

At the April 11th meeting, the board rejected Greta's proposal for three management committee members. They did request that she hire a subordinate finance/administration manager and also a new sales/marketing manager. Excerpts from the board minutes are presented in **Exhibit 2.**

A week later, Greta asked Dr. Karl Tappe, a lawyer who was an old family friend, if he could help. Dr. Tappe had once worked as counsel for a company which had business dealings with Precista. He said that he would try to help if Mr. Huebel wanted him to do so. According to Greta:

> I went to my father and said that I thought we shouldn't argue any more and that we should talk with each other, but that we were having a hard time doing that. I proposed that we ask Dr. Tappe, and my father said, "Yes, I like him, but before we do that, I have to talk with Mami."

> I think that that was really the turning point for me. Until then, I knew that my father had never, never, in his whole life asked my mother for any advice, especially in business things. He always did only what he wanted to do.

> Two days later, he called me into the office and said that he'd talked with my mother and with the other two members on the board. The two men said that if we had that talk with Dr. Tappe, they would resign from the board, and he said, "And you know what that means. " I said, yes, but I asked him to call Dr. Tappe and say that he didn't want to have this talk. He did call and say that he didn't want anyone else involved in this situation, but that he would appreciate it if Dr. Tappe would talk with me, and that he could send the bill to my father. And that was it. I don't think that my father even talked with the other directors. He just made it up.

Mr. and Mrs. Huebel's Responses

During her time at the Owner President Program in May of 1986, Greta Huebel received the following separate letters from her father and mother.

May 9, 1986

Dear Greta:

Mami and I have read your letter of April 30th. There are just the two of us who know about it. We think that you should really think everything over again—really very quietly. When you return from the U.S., you should give us your final decision.

Love,
Mami and Dad

* * * * *

May 13, 1986

My Dear Greta:

To write you my promised letter, I am once more using my beloved little typewriter. Hopefully, you don't mind. I still don't know how to make the new one work—you know changes are not so easy to do at my age. Dad and I were very pleased to get your phone call. It was good to hear your voice. We haven't waited so anxiously for a phone call for a very long time. We hope that the course is a good one and watch, with a lot of respect, your taking on another work load. We really hope that you enjoy this time of studying.

Papi and I were very sad about your letter. We haven't talked a lot about it. We kept it to ourselves. At least once each day I can feel how he is worried—really worried—seriously.

As he did, you have worked very hard, my dear Greta, for Precista. It is not a gamble, we all know. Would selling the company be the answer to the struggle?

The crisis with "the good old man" is not over, and it will not be for awhile. But I really do hope we find a solution. It really makes no sense to think of selling after you have both given everything you have—not for your father and not for you, my dear Greta.

Yes, it is true. Too many things are depending upon you. It is more than time to make changes. All of the struggles with Papi, with the board members, and most probably with the personnel, have ruined your nerves—well how could it be any different? You need time until you are really in your good old form again—in good health—and I think that you should be given that time.

I would be really sorry if you couldn't find a way—especially being surrounded by so many "smart men." Just give them some time. (I personally don't think that it does them any harm to be left in the dark for some time. They don't know that.)

Try not to over challenge yourself. I know that it is easier to write than to do. I wish you strength for your decisions. Papi and I want only the very best for you.

Right now, I won't give this letter to Dad to read. With all of my dear wishes and love.

Mami

Exhibit 1   Excerpts from Board of Directors Meeting Minutes of November 24, 1985

Point 6.2.

The analysis by Mr. Huebel shows that Mr. Schmeed has neglected or not fulfilled the following tasks according to the organization rules, Article 5.

- To give clear orders to the department heads so as to
- provide appropriate controls.
- To guarantee an appropriate personnel structure.
- Introducing cooperative management.
- Regularly informing the board and chairman of the board.

These observations are based upon the following facts:

1. The management committee is not functioning well.

2. The high cost of introducing the latest new product, which did not function well at all, shows that management is not working well together.

3. Motivation among employees is not high. It begins with a lack of information. Mr. Schmeed, despite mutual agreements, is not improving this. Nor can we overlook the fact that Mr. Schmeed gave instructions to the development department without consulting the chief engineer. If this were to continue, Precista could be in great danger. It is important not to lose any of our talented staff nor to have them frustrated.

4. The chairman [Mr. Huebel] is not able to exercise appropriate controls, because Mr. Schmeed does not provide appropriate information.

Point 6.3.

The obvious key to this problem is that Mr. Schmeed is, by his nature, a rather introverted and not very communicative person. This leads to too many miscommunications. The situation will not improve.

Point 6.4.

The Board unanimously votes that the chairman should tell Mr. Schmeed that Precista will fulfill his contract until the end of 1986, but will immediately release him from the position of general manager.

(Five other points covered severance arrangement details.)

Exhibit 2   Excerpts from Board of Directors Meeting Minutes of April 11, 1986 Meeting

Point 7: Organization

Greta Huebel submitted organization Plan #1 again, even though we had decided to go for Plan #2 at the November 24th meeting. We can't see any need for a change to Plan #1.

There were no other formal resolutions, but from the discussion, it can be stated that:

a)   Mr. Huebel, Dr. Riegel, and Dr. Hausman don't think we need a separate Finance and Administration manager who would also be on the management committee. . . . Finance and Administration has to be managed by G. Huebel, and is so represented on the management committee. On the other hand, G. Huebel should be allowed to get a F&A manager whom she thinks is capable for the task.

b)   The gentlemen (Huebel, Riegel, and Hausman) are also convinced that the Marketing and Sales position has to be held by an experienced person—an engineer who has an understanding of marketing. This does not mean that G. Huebel will not have anything to do with marketing and sales. Her position as the chairperson of the management committee gives her enough room to get involved in any questions concerned with marketing.

c)   Besides being chairperson of the management committee, there are more than enough responsibilities for her in the field of Finance and Administration.

d)   G. Huebel is asked to give her opinions on the above proposal. She will do so, and at the same time consider looking for a position and a career in another enterprise.

Precista Tools AG (B)

Greta Huebel returned to Glarus, Switzerland, in late May 1986, after the first three-week phase of the Owner President Management Program at the Harvard Business School. She had asked a friend to meet her at the airport rather than being met by her parents. About a week later, she sent the following letter to the Board of Directors of Precista Tools AG.

To the Members of the Board of Precista Tools AG:

Mr. Franz Huebel
Mrs. Sophie Huebel
Dr. Gert Hausman
Dr. Auguste Riegel

Confidential

Glarus. June 5, 1986

Dear Friends:

The leadership problem in Precista AG has reached a critical stage. We as board members have the responsibility to solve these problems as quickly and as well as possible.

I take the liberty, as a member of the board and at present still as managing director, to set forth my view. It will then be your responsibility to find a solution in the best interests of the company.

As of January 1, 1986, the board appointed me managing director. I accepted this task with enthusiasm and commitment. Very soon, however, I realized that the board would not give me the support and confidence which I needed in order to permit me to perform my functions successfully. I don't blame you for having no confidence: confidence cannot be commanded. It is, however, incomprehensible to me why you, nevertheless, appointed me managing director.

In these last weeks, I have attempted to clarify the situation. With my letter of April 30, 1986 to my father, I expressed my readiness to resign from my job at Precista AG. Later on, I asked him for an exchange of views in the presence of a third

---

A former OPM (Owner President Management Program) participant and Professor Louis B. Barnes wrote this case as a basis for class discussion rather than to illustrate either effective or ineffective handling of an administrative situation.

1

person, Dr. Tappe. This proposal apparently met a negative reaction from other members of the board. The exchange of views never took place.

Thus, the board has created an untenable situation for the company. It is its duty to immediately take a clear decision. I see the two following alternatives:

1. The board accepts my resignation. If this occurs, I wish a separation in friendship and mutual agreement. I am ready to offer my services to the company during a transition period.

2. The board refuses to accept my resignation and confirms me in my job as managing director. I will only accept this solution if a satisfactory situation is created, and, in particular, the following requirements are met:

   a) Clear rules and responsibilities for everyone.
   b) There is a restoration of trust between the board and myself.
   c) A person within whom I have confidence is added to the board.

I kindly ask you for your reply by June 30, 1986. I am willing to continue my job until that date.

With kind regards,

Greta Huebel

That weekend, Mr. and Mrs. Huebel called a meeting of Peter Huebel and his two older sisters to discuss the future of the family business. Greta Huebel was not invited to the meeting.

On July 4th, Mr. Huebel called a board meeting. Peter Huebel was also invited to this meeting. As Greta recalled:

I was very upset that they had all met without me several weeks earlier. I again offered to resign, saying to my father that we had differences of opinion and that it was his company to run as he wanted. I said that for what I'd been doing this past month, I didn't need to be a managing director. It was a half-day's job I was now doing. My proposal was to leave the company, working a half day until he found another solution.

That was it.

On July 7, Franz died of massive heart attack. women in family blamed Greta. Greta owned the will 50% plus her share that was divided between siblings.

Dethroning the King: The Hostile Takeover of Anheuser –Busch, An American Icon
By Julie Macintosh

Workshop

1. **Overview of the Family Dynamics**
    a. **August II**
    b. **August III**
    c. **August 1V**

2. **Overview of the Business**

3. **Breakdown Issues that this case raised for you**
    a. **General Business Issues**
    b. **Leadership/ Succession Issues**
    c. **Ownership/Succession Issues**

4. **Prioritize – Most Critical Issues, drawing potential links between: Leadership; Management; Growth; Profitability; Succession**

5. **How could these issues have been handled differently? What could have been done to better resolve this situation?**

6. **Application: What can you learn from this Case Study?**

Bequeathing your most important assets

An ethical will is an ancient tradition that can help prevent the strife that often occurs in modern families after the death of a family business leader.

By Alan G. Weinstein and Scott E. Friedman

Estate planning may well be the most traditional financial planning exercise in the U.S., and perhaps the best-known of all legal documents is the will -- the instrument by which individuals direct how and to whom their material assets are to be transferred upon their death. Although considerable thought enters into the typical estate-planning process, many wills completely ignore the two most important assets of all: (1) insight and rationale as to why certain decisions were made, including why certain assets were transferred to designated beneficiaries; and (2) "wealth" as measured by wisdom, insight and dearly held beliefs.

The pressing need for a more holistic approach to estate planning could not be any clearer. We have worked with many family businesses over the years that have experienced the death of a leader who had not thought to transfer his or her intentions, wishes and wisdom to the surviving family members. The results are often traumatic. We have seen families and their businesses unravel and implode. We have seen every kind of intra-family litigation, including sibling suing sibling and children suing parents.

In the storm of controversy and resulting despair, the refrain among survivors is as predictable as the sun rising in the east: "What would Dad [Mom] have wanted?" Without the benefit of clear guidance, each child freely interprets the wishes of the deceased parent. As a result, offspring often bicker and seek to promote their own self-interest, to the detriment of the family business and family relationships.

Fortunately, there is a way to prevent such tragedies. An ancient but little-publicized tool known as an "ethical will" in effect can help guide surviving family members through difficult times and dilemmas.

An ethical will has its roots in the Bible. Jacob gathered his twelve children and instructed them on how they should conduct their affairs after he died. In modern times, the ethical will is most typically prepared as a letter to loved ones, written with the intention of passing on wisdom, values and expressions of feelings that are not easily expressed face to face.

An ethical will can be used by anyone who seeks to (1) share his or her intentions with regard to leadership, succession, ownership and governance of the family business; and (2) provide a moral compass that permits the leader to transmit his or her insights and wisdom to the next generation.

There is almost no limit to the amount or type of information that can be included in this document. An ethical will is a vehicle for expressing your deeply held personal or family values, visions and beliefs gleaned from a lifetime of learning and experiences, both good and bad.

Adjunct to a succession plan

While traditional estate or succession plans might detail transfer of ownership interests in operating businesses, an ethical will might explain why you are transferring the interests in this way. It could also outline how you hope future decisions regarding the company's operations might be made in order to build collaboration and family unity.

An ethical will can be prepared with a view toward creating a higher level of cooperation among family or group members who often struggle in the vacuum created by a leader's passing. Families in business together, prone to losing direction and turning toward the negative emotions of selfishness, resentment and jealousy, might find invaluable benefits from the legacy of insight and wishes passed on by the patriarch or matriarch.

Ethical wills are multifaceted tools that can be used to transmit not just your intentions but, equally important, your thoughts and feelings on innumerable subjects, some of which might be too difficult to express directly while you're alive. For example, your greatest moments of triumph -- or failure -- and the lessons learned from the experience can be shared without embarrassment. The lessons might suggest or amplify core principles and values that you've learned and wish to pass along.

Less specific guidance, such as a list of formal and informal advisers, may be offered in a section of the ethical will. Another section, perhaps called "Recommended Reading," might list influential books and other reading material that helped shape your decisions.

You might wish to consider describing a particularly memorable trip or other special experience. Family members who read the passage will recall a beautiful moment with a smile and a sense of understanding about the real lessons learned from that moment.

In your own unique way, you can use an ethical will to create a lasting legacy of wisdom and insight that survivors might incorporate as a framework for living a rich and rewarding life.

Collapse in a family business

Not long ago, one of us counseled a company that underwent a management transition when the patriarch died suddenly. Three sons and two daughters worked in the business, which the father had ruled with an iron fist. The father loved his children and had always planned for them to take over the business upon his retirement. Unfortunately, his unexpected death left the family unprepared for a smooth succession of business leadership.

The mother, who inherited legal ownership of the business, did her best to keep peace in the family, but the children bickered. The sons, who already had stronger leadership roles in the business, convinced their mother to give them even more leadership responsibility. Ultimately, the family business broke apart and the daughters left to start their own competing company. Holidays were never the same after that, and the mother passed away brokenhearted.

Without an ethical will to provide clear guidance of the father's intentions, the three sons were able to prevail upon their mother to grant them virtually unlimited authority to run the family business as they saw fit. The daughters felt their father's intentions were being violated and that leadership and management of the family business should have been shared equally by all five siblings. The daughters accused their mother of favoring her three sons.

The father's silence on leadership succession in this family business created a vacuum that promoted his children's focus on their own self-interest. His wishes and intentions as the founder died with him.

Sam Steinberg, founder of the Steinberg Supermarket chain of Montreal, Canada, was another family business leader who apparently failed to communicate clear expectations about how his company would operate after his death. In that family business, the lack of a clear succession plan -- which might have been included in an ethical will -- led to well-documented intra-family discord and litigation. One company executive, commenting on the succession plan and implicitly recognizing the confusion over the founder's intentions, observed that after Steinberg's death, his daughter Mitzi and her husband "really took hold. *This must have been his desire.* If you get to be 70 and you haven't planned for the succession of the business, then this must be what you want. He knew he had a heart problem, and his brother died in his 50s. So ..." (see Sam Steinberg Case, Harvard Business School 9-392-061, rev. March 10, 1993. Italics added).

This executive's observations may have been accurate. But we can't help believing that Sam Steinberg's family would have been better off if his intentions had been explicitly spelled out and shared with his relatives and key company executives.

Such disasters occur every day in family businesses around the world. Sometimes, the leader's intentions were clear but never communicated to his survivors. Other times, the leader simply ignored the difficult planning decisions that inevitably arise. In either case, the surviving family members are left with little guidance about how to lead the company.

Guiding principles

CEO Paul Ciminelli of Ciminelli Development Company, a successful family-owned real estate development business headquartered in western New York, has written an ethical will. Ciminelli, a second-generation leader, says his main purpose in preparing this document is to help explain to his children how he has chosen to live his life. "I wanted to let my sons know what guided me through my life," explains Ciminelli, a second-generation leader.

In his ethical will, Ciminelli expresses his values and core principles and explains the background behind some of the most important decisions he has made in his life. His approach is decidedly not about trying to convince his children to mimic his decisions. To the contrary, he uses his life choices to set the stage for his children to better explore their own path. Among other subjects, he discusses the importance of finding balance in life, his relationship with his own father and why he decided to pursue a career in his family business.

Although Ciminelli chose to enter the family firm, he makes it clear that his children need not feel obligated to do the same. If they want to join the business, he has set up ground rules that specify education and outside business experience as prerequisites. His ethical will, he explains, gives him a reference point in transferring his values to his children. He wants to deal with his children as people, not just legal beneficiaries of material wealth. Ciminelli, a student of leadership and business, wants to transfer his most important lessons and experiences, not just a portfolio full of real estate projects, to his children.

Preparation tips

While there is no right or wrong way to prepare an ethical will, we offer a few recommendations based on our experiences. Traditionally, an ethical will is provided to its intended recipients upon the author's death. We believe a better approach is to review the document as a family while the author is still alive. This creates a better learning opportunity for the beneficiaries, who can ask questions and gain a sense of clarity and understanding.

As is done with traditional wills, it can be useful to update and edit the ethical will and perhaps add to it over the years as you continue to clarify your thoughts, knowledge and insight.

Consider using communication options such as videotape, CD or DVD. A statement that captures not just your words, but also your tone, emotions and other intangibles, can be extremely helpful to your beneficiaries. If you're prepared to spend time and money on recording family events over the years -- school plays, athletic contests, holiday celebrations, barbecues -- it makes sense to also invest resources in recording your insights and intentions.

Finally, we note that an ethical will, although potentially more valuable than a traditional will, may rarely if ever be considered a legally enforceable instrument. If there are particular points you would prefer to make enforceable, it's advisable to discuss them with legal counsel.

Sharing your wisdom

As the cliché goes, it's better to teach a person how to fish than to give a person a fish. The logic is compelling: Education creates self-sufficiency; material gifts risk breeding dependency. Since parents live with the constant awareness that they won't always be around to take care of their children, their insight, knowledge and self-sufficiency are clearly the most important assets they can transfer. Yet in the traditional will, we focus on how many fish (read: money and tangible assets) we can give away. The ethical will offers a wonderful platform to share insight and wisdom with children, friends and favorite organizations. We encourage everyone to consider taking advantage of this opportunity.   FB

Alan G. Weinstein (agw@canisius.edu) has been a coach to CEOs, a college professor, a family business consultant and an entrepreneur. He holds a professorship in management and entrepreneurship at the Wehle School of Business, Canisius College, Buffalo, N.Y. He grew up in a family business and regularly teaches courses in family business management. Scott E. Friedman (sfriedman@lippes.com), a managing partner at Lippes Mathias Wexler Friedman LLP, a law firm in Buffalo, N.Y., consults with family businesses across the U.S. He has written several books and numerous articles on family business and is co-author of the upcoming book Secrets from the Delphi Café: Unlocking the Code to Happiness.

ORAL COMMUNICATION RUBRIC

SAN DIEGO STATE UNIVERSITY

College of Business Administration

If this rubric is used to assign grades, the instructor will:

1. Decide how to weight the criteria (equal weight or otherwise).

2. Assign points to each of the three categories – this could be as simple as 1, 2, 3 for the categories or may allow for a range within categories (for example Below Expectations will be 0-1, Meets Expectations will be 2-3, Exceeds Expectations will be 4-5). Differing point ranges may be assigned in the categories. For example, a point system that translates directly to a 100% grade scale might give the Below Expectations a bigger range (0-6) with Meets Expectations a 7-8 and Exceeds Expectations a 9-10.

3. Complete a copy of the rubric for each student and compute the weighted score for the student.

	Below Expectations	Meets Expectations	Exceeds Expectations	POINTS
Organization	No opening and/or closing statements or irrelevant opening/closing statements. Loses focus more than once. Does not manage time effectively. No logical sequence of information. Mechanistic.	Offers some type of opening and closing statements. Follows logical sequence but structure could be better. May need more elaboration on one or more points. Adequate time management, but could be stronger.	Clear opening and closing statements. Catches audience's interest, provides overview/conclusion. Follows logical sequence, stays focused, good explanations. Effective time management and strong transitions. Strong mental take away for audience.	___
Voice Quality & Pace	Mumbles, mispronounces words, grammatical errors, "umms". Difficult to understand. Speaks too quietly or too loudly. Speaks too fast or too slow. Loses train of thought, tentative. Lacks enthusiasm.	Easily understood. Speaks loud enough to be heard and at appropriate pace. Some awkward pauses or halting delivery but mostly clear and natural. Could display greater enthusiasm, seem more genuinely interested in own presentation.	Enthusiastic and engaging. Speaks clearly and loudly enough at a comfortable pace. Exudes confidence and interest. No grammatical or pronunciation errors. Presentation appears conversational, extemporaneous, and natural.	___
Mannerisms & Body Language	Demonstrates distracting mannerisms which may include bad posture, shifting feet, too much or too little hand movement. Body language reveals reluctance to interact with audience. Seems fearful/very nervous.	No significantly distracting mannerisms. Acceptable posture. Body language mostly demonstrates comfort in interacting with audience but occasional instances of discomfort may be communicated. Seems natural for the most part.	Body language used effectively to maintain audience's interest. Body language reflects presenter's reaction to, and empathy with, the audience. Gestures match verbal content, are comfortable and relaxed, seem spontaneous.	
Professionalism & Appearance	Does not meet minimum requirements for business dress. Makes excuses for aspects of the presentation. Inappropriate word choice for audience. Inappropriately informal.	Meets minimum standards for business dress and appearance. Generally treats audience professionally, acceptable word choice (no slang). May seem to lack confidence at times. Reasonably credible.	Dressed appropriately. Appearance engenders respect and credibility. Treats audience professionally. Speaker appears confident and has good command of the topic.	
Rapport with Audience & Use of Media	Does not connect with audience. Little to no eye contact. Reads heavily on slides and/or notes. Attempts to cover too many slides or lingers too long on too few slides.	Tries to maintain eye contact most of the time but instances may be fleeting in length. Scans the room. Some reliance on notes or slides.	Genuinely connects with audience. Maintains eye contact throughout. Visuals (slides, etc.) effortlessly enhance speech.	___

GRAND TOTAL: ___

Updated January 2009
Credits: This document borrows from the SPEAKS Rubric from CSU-Fullerton Business Communication Program and the CSU-Chico, College of Business Oral Communication Rubric.

WRITTEN COMMUNICATION RUBRIC

SAN DIEGO STATE UNIVERSITY

College of Business Administration

If this rubric is used to assign grades, the instructor will:

1. Decide how to weight the criteria (equal weight or otherwise).
2. Assign points to each of the three categories – this could be as simple as 1, 2, 3 for the categories or may allow for a range within categories (for example Below Expectations will be 0-1, Meets Expectations will be 2-3, Exceeds Expectations will be 4-5). Differing point ranges may be assigned in the categories. For example, a point system that translates directly to a 100% grade scale might give the Below Expectations a bigger range (0-6) with Meets Expectations a 7-8 and Exceeds Expectations 9-10.
3. Complete a copy of the rubric for each student and compute the weighted score for the student.

	Below Expectations	Meets Expectations	Exceeds Expectations	POINTS
Content	Does not adequately cover the assigned task. The primary thesis may not be clear or if it is, little topic development is evident. Assertions made in the writing are either weakly supported or no support is offered.	The assigned task is covered sufficiently. The primary thesis is clear but there is some room for further development of the topic. Support is offered for assertions that are made but that support could be stronger, more compelling or more inclusive of all issues.	The assigned task is thoroughly covered and completed. The primary thesis is clear and fully developed. Assertions made throughout the writing are compelling and clearly supported.	___
Organization	Paper lacks logical sequence hence causing format to interfere with readability. Does not use proper paragraphing. Topic sentences do not lead to rest of paragraph or are missing altogether.	Paper follows logical sequence with identifiable beginning, development, and conclusion. Generally proper use of paragraph structure and topic sentences. Organization and/or headings help the reader to follow and find information.	Paper flows well with appropriate beginning, development, and conclusion. Paragraph structure contributes to flow and transitions. Organization and/or headings help the reader to understand and remember information.	___
Audience	Writer is internally focused rather than focused on the reader. No clear awareness or understanding of the audience is evident. Writer may appear discourteous to the reader.	Writer acknowledges the reader and displays some thought about the nature of the audience. Reader is treated politely and positively. No evidence of inappropriate attitude.	Writer clearly focuses writing to the audience, and displays empathy for the reader. Goodwill is created through consideration of the reader's needs. Message tailored directly for the reader.	
Style	Overuse of simple sentences. May misuse words or idioms. May include slang. Wordy rather than concise. Writing shows lack of sophistication or variety in vocabulary. Awkward. Little or no use of business terms.	Sentences vary in length and style. Strong action verbs are used. Occasionally uses jargon or clichés. Vocabulary and word usage generally is correct and shows some variety. Uses business terms appropriately.	Demonstrates a sophisticated grasp of the language in terms of both sentence structure and vocabulary. Writes fluidly and concisely. Includes appropriate business terms.	___
Mechanics	Significant errors in word usage, sentence structure (run-ons, fragments), spelling, punctuation, and capitalization. Errors undermine credibility of content and readability.	Relatively free of errors in word usage, sentence structure (run-ons, fragments), spelling, punctuation, and capitalization. Mechanics do not detract from credibility of the content.	No errors in word usage, sentence structure (run-ons, fragments), spelling, punctuation, and capitalization. Strong mechanics help to establish credibility.	___
Referencing	References (if called for) are missing or do not use correct referencing style.	Generally correct referencing (if called for) using APA or MLA style.	References (if called for) are consistently correct using APA or MLA style. No missing citations.	

GRAND TOTAL: _____

Updated January 2009
Credits: This document borrows from the SDSU IDS Department Written Skills Rubric (Vik, Reinig, Anderson-Cruz); the IDS Upper Division Writing Assessment Rubric, and the CLASS Rubric from CSU-Fullerton (Fraser, et. al., 2005).